The Gift

Other books by Echo Bodine

Hands That Heal
Echoes of the Soul
Relax, It's Only a Ghost
A Still, Small Voice
Dear Echo

The Gift

*Understand and Develop Your
Psychic Abilities*

Echo Bodine

NEW WORLD LIBRARY
NOVATO, CALIFORNIA

New World Library
14 Pamaron Way
Novato, California 94949

Copyright © 2003 by Echo L. Bodine

Cover design: Knockout Design / Peri Poloni Designer
Text design: Tona Pearce Myers

Library of Congress Cataloging-in-Publication Data
Bodine, Echo L.
The gift : understand and develop your psychic abilities / Echo L. Bodine.
        p.   cm.
Includes bibliographical references.
ISBN 1-57731-205-8 (alk. paper)
    1. Psychic ability. I. Title.
BF1031 .B612   2003
133.8—dc21   2002014134

First Printing, February 2003
ISBN 1-57731-205-8
Printed in Canada on acid-free, partially recycled paper
Distributed to the trade by Publishers Group West

10 9 8 7 6 5 4

Dedication

I would like to dedicate this book to
all the wonderful role models we have today who
have shown us what Jesus meant
when he said, "These gifts I give unto you,
and greater works shall you do."
Thank you for not letting
the fears and ignorance of the world
keep you from doing your work
and for showing all of us
what is possible.
Rosemary Altea
George Anderson
Sylvia Browne
John Edward
Char Margolis
James Van Praagh
And to the most important role model in my life,
my brother and teacher
Rabbi Jeshua ben Joseph.

Contents

Foreword
by Melody Beattie

The woman gazed into her crystal ball, then solemnly looked at Echo and me.

"I see, I see...."

Echo and I leaned forward anxiously.

"I see you two playing the piano at a recital, then afterwards having Kool-aid and cookies."

We paid her $10, then rushed to the car to giggle and talk about our latest reading.

In many ways, this little tidbit about the piano recitals was more believable than what another, more accurate psychic had predicted for both of us: that we would go on to become writers and teachers, and our names would be known worldwide.

The year was 1975. Psychic phenomena for the most part was still underground. Echo and I had instantly become best friends when we'd met, a year earlier. Echo was the first psychic I had ever met and one of our mutual passions became going to visit psychics. For different reasons, we were both intrigued by this mysterious world beyond and the information transmitted from it to us.

Echo had been raised in a normal family transformed by a paranormal experience in 1965. From then on, auras, listening to what spirit had to say, and trusting intuition became as everyday to her as vacuum cleaners and grocery lists are to most of us. I didn't have a clue what any of this was about. Nor did I know how it fit into my religious upbringing — which included Baptist Bible summer camps, Covenant Christian High School Academy, thousands of Methodist Sunday school classes, and weekly church services.

Like most people, I had psychic experiences that ranged from hearing clear guidance in the form of thoughts that weren't my own (clairaudience) to being able to get a radar-type feeling for situations I was about to walk into (clairsentience), but I didn't have the words to describe these incidents and lacked the training to understand them.

Over the years — just as predicted — Echo went on to become an internationally renowned psychic and healer and the author of many books on these subjects (although the piano recital has yet to take place).

How do you tell an accurate psychic from an inaccurate one? What can you reasonably expect from a reading? When is it time to get a reading and, just as importantly, when is it the wrong time? What's a third eye, and how do you open it? How can you see and hear things invisible to our physical eyes and not audible to our ears? How do you accurately interpret the things you see and hear, especially when your own fears, hopes, and dreams get in the way? Are we all psychic, or just a handful of us? Is it wrong to pursue psychic phenomenon, or is it an integral part of spirituality and spiritual growth?

Echo has mentored me and thousands of others who want to learn more about this mysterious otherworld and information communicated to us from it. Sometimes she's given us answers and suggestions; other times she's encouraged us to discover our own answers (as any good mentor does). More importantly, besides telling us how to grow psychically, she's given us the belief that we can.

There's a doorway, a gate, that stands before us. See, it's started to swing open. Maybe you've had that sense of knowing who was going to call before the phone rang. Maybe you've seen pictures flash through your mind, like scenes in a slide show. Or maybe, like the boy in the movie *Sixth Sense,* you can see and hear dead people.

You don't have to hang a shingle and become a professional psychic to grow and develop psychically. Learning to communicate with the world beyond can be helpful in building and maintaining personal relationships, in the business world, in our personal growth, and in being of true service to others. I've found psychic abilities invaluable in the creative process. From what to get someone for a birthday gift to what to write about next — and how to write it — there's a wealth of information out there waiting for us to tap into it.

As we roll into and through the twenty-first century, more and more people are finding themselves standing at this gateway. We're heading toward a time when auras, intuition, and spirit guides will be household words almost as common as *computers,* and as helpful for navigating our way through life. The veil between the worlds has thinned. As many seers have prophesized, we stand at the brink of a creative and spiritual revolution that includes the everyday use of psychic information.

Without hesitation, I can tell you that Echo Lee Bodine is one of the keepers of information for people crossing this threshold. She was trained and taught during a time when only a select few had this information (or access to it), and most of it was passed on through oral teaching and hands-on practice. Most of her teachers have passed over or retired. Now, this information is finally offered to the masses.

I've watched Echo come up through the ranks and become established as a psychic and healer the old-fashioned way: by paying dues, perfecting her abilities, and spending time being a student before she moved into the position of teacher.

Before embarking on a recent trip to Tibet, my hiking partner and I talked about our goals and our hopes and dreams for this trip. He wanted to see the terrain, and the people, and visit the holy Mount Kailash. Without reservation, I told him what I wanted: to go to the next level with my psychic abilities.

If you're ready to make your psychic and spiritual practice deliberate and conscious instead of random, you don't have to go to Tibet. This is the book for you. If you're looking for a quick fix, how to become psychic overnight, this may not be the book for you — or on second thought, maybe it is. Come join Echo while she teaches what she has passed on to me and countless others: psychic development is a skill like any other that takes practice to hone. Using our sixth sense can become as natural as using any of our other senses —smell, sight, hearing, touch, or taste — but it takes time, patience, and correct spiritual attitudes and discipline. And using our sixth sense is no more taboo than using our physical eyes or ears.

It's a heavenly gift. What follows is an excellent, down-to-earth operator/owner instruction manual on how to use it.

Acknowledgments

This book has been in the making for years. There has been so much that I needed to learn along the way besides my psychic development, and I have several people to thank:

Eve Olson, for opening the door, for her psychic guidance in helping me come to terms with these gifts, and for her patience as I worked through all my resistance.

My teacher Birdie Torgeson, who spent countless hours helping me understand and develop these gifts.

My gifted psychic family.

My son, Kurt, for all your help on the Bible research.

My students.

As always, my wonderful chiropractor and friend, Dr. Marcie New, for keeping my body in alignment and healthy while I worked on the book.

Georgia Hughes, for letting me push the deadline until I got it right and for the fabulous brownies that helped me meet the deadline!

My boyfriend, Mike Hartley, who never complained once about all the rewrites or time I spent away from "our time."

To my very dear friend Melody Beattie, for writing the foreword.

And to Munro Magruder and Marjorie Conte, for all the work they're now going to do to get this book out into the world.

Introduction

The first time I remember being aware of someone with psychic abilities was when I was a young girl and I saw the classic horror movie *The Wolf Man*. In the film, an old toothless gypsy fortune teller advises the bitten Lon Chaney Jr. about the power of the full moon. She has a very old, wrinkled face and a far-off gaze, as if she were always *seeing* something awful and foreboding. Just looking at her gave me the willies, and from then on she embodied what I thought psychics were. Still today, even though Hollywood no longer portrays psychically gifted people this way, the old stereotype remains an illusive popular image.

In the fall of 1965, we had a very unusual experience in my family. One of my brothers had a terrifying experience of seeing a white figure floating through a room. Since we were "mainstream Presbyterians," we had no idea what to make of this, so Mom called around to some of her friends to see if anyone could refer her to a psychic. She got the name and number of a psychic/medium living in St. Paul,

Minnesota, and she gave her a call. The psychic told her that this had happened for a reason, that Mom and all four of us kids had some unusual gifts, and that she wanted to see us for a psychic reading. Mom's immediate response was that we needed to think it over and told the psychic that we'd get back to her. By the next day, we were so curious about what she said that Mom called her back and scheduled appointments for both of us.

I was seventeen years old and very nervous about seeing a psychic. I had no idea what to expect and assumed she would be your typical gypsy fortune teller—toothless, with gold hoop earrings and long dangling scarves, staring into a crystal ball or reading your palm. I was pleasantly surprised to find just the opposite. She was a very sweet, gentle woman from England who looked more like she belonged on Waltons Mountain than in some werewolf movie. I wondered if she would know all my deep dark secrets and when I was going to die, but as it turned out, she knew neither. Instead, she told me that I was born with psychic abilities and the gift of healing. She said that I had come here in this lifetime to develop my abilities and then to teach others how to develop theirs.

I was not very happy with this information, and I told her that I didn't have any psychic abilities. My plan was to have a "normal" life. Go to college, get married, and have a bunch of kids. But she said that my *soul* had a different plan. She said I had been adjusting to my psychic abilities ever since I was a little girl and had gotten used to them. I had no idea what this woman was talking about, but I did know one thing for certain. I didn't want to be an old toothless gypsy fortune teller, and it frightened me to think that that's what my "soul's plan" was.

So much has happened since that fate-filled night back in 1965. I took psychic development classes for two years while I attended the University of Minnesota. I practiced doing mini-readings and healings on friends and acquaintances while I worked in mainstream jobs for twelve years. After several synchronistic experiences with the Universe pushing me in this direction, I became a professional psychic, healer, and teacher, though I'm happy to say that my life has no resemblance to the wandering gypsies in the movies. Since 1979 I've been doing psychic readings and spiritual healing, teaching healing and psychic development classes, writing books, and traveling around the country giving lectures. For two years, I had my own cable TV show, and I've been a featured guest on numerous television and radio programs.

The Journey Thirty-Five Years Later

Thirty-five years after that first meeting with Mrs. Olson, and three days before Easter, my minister, Reverend Ken Williamson, asked me to be a guest on his weekly inspirational television show, *Quest for Truth*. The topic was "spiritual gifts," and he wanted me to talk about my journey as a spiritual healer and psychic. Up until this point, my only involvement in his show was always behind the scenes. Everyone who ran a camera or helped produce the show was a member of Reverend Williamson's congregation at Unity South Church, and everyone knew what I did for a living. But I was nervous about doing the show because of the young man who ran the production studio. He had made it clear to all of us that he was a *Christian,* and many times he had made comments that he thought people in the *New Age* movement were wrong or misled. I really liked this young man and didn't want to jeopardize our working relationship, so for months I had made a point of not talking about my career.

I'm a Christian myself, but my beliefs and other Christians' beliefs about psychic gifts seem to be quite different. Somewhere along the line, I stopped getting into discussions about these abilities with religious people, particularly those who were *forthright* about being Christian, because the conversations seemed futile, and I grew tired of always feeling like I had to defend my psychic gifts.

My stomach was in knots as Reverend Williamson started the show. I kept telling myself not to make one person's opinion so important—that if I had to lose one more person in my life because of these abilities, so be it. I had to be true to myself and the path I came here to walk. For some reason, I wasn't doing such a good job of convincing myself that this young man's opinion wasn't important.

Reverend Williamson began the interview by asking me what it's like to channel God's healing energy, and he asked if I had witnessed miracles in people's lives. He asked me to talk about how this affected my relationship with God, and he wanted to know if I felt responsible to heal all the sickness in the world. I talked about the inner voice that guides me and helps me discern who to work on and who not to work on, and I briefly shared a couple of healing stories. Then the focus shifted to my psychic abilities. He asked me to explain what psychic gifts are and what it was like to have these gifts. We had a great discussion about the gifts of the Holy Spirit that are described in the Bible and how the gift of prophecy is the same thing that we now call "psychic abilities." Finally, Reverend Williamson asked me what was the hardest part about having these gifts, and I said it was my frustration with the Christian community—since many of them label these gifts as "evil," and this attitude keeps them and many others from properly understanding what these God-given gifts really are.

The show turned out to be a turning point in my life. When it was over, the crew and my minister said they were very moved by what I had to say, and yet as grateful as I was to hear their comments, I still had this young man in the back of my mind. I knew there was no way we could ignore our differences anymore, and so I walked to the control room and asked him point-blank if he was upset with me. Not only was he not angry, he said he felt like he wanted to apologize for all the people who have been mean to me over the years, and that because of the way I explained my gifts, he now saw them in a different light. In fact, he wanted to show his pastor a copy of the program to help him see these gifts from a different perspective as well. I was very touched by what he said, and I felt something inside of me heal in that short five-minute conversation. I wanted to hug him for his loving response but felt I should just leave it alone. We were both visibly moved by the experience.

Over the next couple of days, an important shift took place inside of me, though I didn't understand the extent of it until Easter morning, when I was getting ready for church. I was looking in the mirror, putting on my makeup, when I had a psychic vision of Jesus standing behind me. This in itself didn't startle me because he has appeared to me many times throughout my life. Sometimes it has been to help me get through a personal crisis; other times to teach me about healing by the laying on of hands. This time his visit concerned neither of these. He told me that psychic abilities are one of the gifts of the Spirit and that this gift comes from God. He said that when he was alive he was persecuted for, among many things, having these gifts and that he had hoped in the thousands of years since his death that our consciousness about them would have changed. He said all religious leaders should be developing their psychic gifts and teaching these abilities in their churches and synagogues. And he told me that the next part of my journey was to help change the consciousness of the planet about psychic abilities. He said psychically gifted people have had to be defensive long enough and that I needed to help educate people so that they would honor these gifts rather than categorize them as wrong or evil.

I looked at him as if to say, "You want me to do what?" And he smiled at me as if to say, "You heard me." With that, he disappeared, and I went to Easter services stunned by his message.

It's been my experience that people fear or judge what they don't understand. My hope with this book is that it will help you understand who psychics are, what their abilities consist of, and how you can recognize and develop your own psychic abilities, which we all possess.

Chapter 1 describes psychics and psychic abilities, and in chapter 2 I address the common questions and misconceptions people have and how to tell the difference between real psychics and scam artists.

Chapter 3 describes what the Bible really has to say about these gifts. Then I explain what I believe Jesus meant when he said "these gifts I give unto you and greater works shall you do."

In chapters 4 through 7, I take you through a step-by-step psychic development course to help you develop and refine your abilities, and I give you strategies for staying grounded and developing boundaries.

In chapter 8, I cover how to live in this world with your psychic abilities and how to avoid some common pitfalls you may run into.

At the end of the book, you will find a list of recommended books and interviews with five gifted psychics, who share their personal stories of how they discovered and developed their gifts.

Whether you persevere in developing your psychic abilities to their fullest or not, I believe this book is important for everyone because it helps demystify psychic gifts, which is the first step to eliminating the fears and judgments that still often surround them.

The Gift

Chapter 1

Psychic Abilities

By hearing ye shall hear, and shall not understand;
and seeing ye shall see, and shall not perceive.

— Matthew 13:14

As I was writing this book, an acquaintance asked me in passing what I was working on. When I told her, she looked at me with this glazed stare and asked me, "Why on earth would anyone want to develop psychic abilities?" For a second, her question took me aback, and then I realized that she probably had no idea how often she uses her own psychic abilities to help her in her everyday life.

Each one of us has psychic abilities to one degree or another, but because they're usually so subtle, we often don't realize that's what we're using. When Mrs. Olson first told me I had these gifts, I didn't have a clue what she was talking about until she was able to explain it in terms I could understand.

Have you ever realized the answer to a question when a picture popped into your head? Has a thought ever come into your head out of nowhere, and it was the guidance you were praying for? Have you ever sensed something about a person that wasn't based on anything you consciously knew but that later turned out to be true? Have you ever experienced a smell that reminded you of a deceased loved one? Every day at least one of our psychic abilities is helping us in some way.

The Four Psychic Gifts

There are four psychic abilities: clairvoyance, clairaudience, clairsentience, and clairgustance. Clairvoyance is the gift of seeing. We all have an invisible third eye located in the middle of our forehead, which is sometimes referred to as the psychic eye. It's with this third eye that a clairvoyant sees information in the form of pictures, visions, or images. When we see a ghost, a spirit guide, or a deceased loved one, that's also clairvoyance.

Clairaudience is the gift of hearing, which sounds simple enough, but it can become quite confusing. When a clairaudient receives information, it comes into his or her mind as thoughts. Since these thoughts don't sound any different than one's own thoughts, the clairaudient's job is to learn, through trial and error, to distinguish between personal thoughts and incoming psychic information.

There are a variety of sources that send thoughts to us and the sources have a lot to do with the path we're on. We could be receiving information from our spirit guides, a guardian angel, deceased loved ones, or earthbound spirits. Spirits do not have voices like we do. The way they communicate with each other and with us is that they project thoughts.

There's a great line in the Steven Spielberg movie *Always* that describes clairaudience. The character played by Richard Dreyfuss is killed in a plane crash, and Audrey Hepburn, who plays an angel, has to explain to him that he's now a spirit guide to another character in the movie. She tells him that the way to communicate with human beings is to send thoughts to them. She says something like, "They always think it's their own thoughts, but that doesn't matter because at least they get the message." This is how our spirit guides and deceased loves ones communicate to us. They send us thoughts to give us guidance. Our souls know where the information is coming from, but we don't become conscious of the true source until we start paying more attention.

Mental Telepathy

One of my favorite aspects of clairaudience is mental telepathy. This is *hearing* the thoughts of people who are either in your general vicinity or simply in your life. It's not uncommon for us to pick up the thoughts of people we are very connected to on a psychic level. My son, with whom I share a very strong psychic connection, can be making ribs for dinner in Lincoln, Nebraska, and I can be sitting in my office in Minneapolis thinking and smelling ribs. Or one of my best friends who lives in California can be fighting the urge to have a hot fudge sundae, and I'll get in my car and go get one. Often, thoughts will come into my mind so strongly and I won't know who or where they're coming from. Only in the last couple of years have I tried to find the sources of some of these powerful random thoughts, and it's been fun to find out just how connected I am to the people in my life.

How many times have you verbalized a thought only to have someone you're with say they were just thinking the same thing? Have you ever had the thought of someone pop into your head and then the phone rang and it was that person? Or have an image of a friend pop into your mind, and within a day or two, you run into him or her? These are simply thoughts that people are sending out. They're thinking of us, and we receive these thoughts on a psychic level without being aware of it. As we grow psychically and spiritually, we become more open to mental telepathy, and it makes life pretty fun.

Clairsentience

The next psychic gift, clairsentience, has to do with sensing. This is more of a body feeling or sensing than actually seeing visions with your third eye or psychically hearing thoughts or voices. If someone is clairsentient, he or she has psychic radar working all the time, psychically feeling the environment as he or she goes through the day. The blue lobster we have in our aquarium at home is a good illustration of a clairsentient. He has long tentacles that reach out in front of his body that scope out the environment as he moves throughout the tank. Clairsentients have this kind of sensing going on in their bodies. They can walk into a room or a meeting and sense the mood. I believe all psychics have this gift and use it their whole life. It's how we survive living in these sensitive bodies. We go into any situation in life and send out our "feelers" because we want to know what kind of environment we're stepping into. The downside to clairsentience is that we can become psychic sponges. We can soak up too much of the environment and carry it with us. I cover this in more detail in chapter 2, where I also give some suggestions for how to create necessary boundaries and distance.

Clairgustance

Clairgustance is the last psychic gift, and it's an odd one. It's the gift of smell. People with clairgustance have a psychic nose, which means they smell things that aren't physically present. For example, one day a client asked me about a used car she was thinking of purchasing. She wanted to know if I felt there was anything wrong with it. I got the strong smell of an overheated engine. Despite this indication of potential trouble, she purchased the car anyway, and as it turned out, she continually had a problem with the engine overheating.

The most common way that clairgustance manifests itself is when a deceased loved one comes to visit us. The person will project a smell to us (by thinking about it), such as the cologne the person used to wear, or something that will immediately bring a thought of the loved one to mind. Once I was doing a reading for a woman, and I got the strong smell of fresh baked bread. Then I had a psychic image of a woman standing on the other side, waving and smiling. She had on an apron, and I saw a picture of an oven. Again I got the smell of baked bread. I asked my client if fresh baked bread and a woman smiling and waving on the other side was significant to her, and she told me her aunt had just died and that, when she was alive, she always baked bread for people. This was simply her aunt's way of saying hello.

The other thing about clairgustance is that the smells don't last long. They're usually a quick whiff and they're gone.

Do all psychics have all these abilities? I think we all have clairsentience, but of the two main gifts, clairvoyance and clairaudience, most psychics have one or the other and some have both. The simplest way that a person can tell which abilities he or she has is by paying attention to the type of information that comes in throughout the day: Is it in the form of thoughts, pictures, sensing, or smells? I tell my beginner students that before they work on accuracy, they first have to determine which gifts they have.

How Psychic Gifts Work

One of the most widespread misunderstandings about psychic gifts is how they work. People in general assume that psychics receive information as if it were a well-written telegram; unfortunately, it doesn't work this way. Clairvoyants, for example, get their information in the form of pictures, images, or visions. Their job is to interpret the pictures accurately, and to do this they must ask questions. Often, professional psychics need help from the clients themselves to properly interpret what the pictures mean. This has led skeptics to claim that psychics don't do anything other than fish for information and then give that information back to the client. What may look like "fishing" to an observer is simply part of the psychic's effort to be as accurate as possible in his or her interpretation.

People often ask me why it is that psychic information doesn't come in clear, laid-out sentences, and all I can tell them is that I wonder about this myself. When spirits communicate to us, they keep it brief and to the point. They don't embellish. Often, information comes in like words in a crossword puzzle, and if we get one word at a time, on its own, it might not mean much at first. We patiently wait for more information to come in order to put the whole message together.

Here's an example: I had a client who had been looking at various office spaces around town to rent. She didn't know which one to rent and asked if I could help her out. I got a picture of an O. I waited for another picture, but nothing else came. I asked her if O meant anything to her. Did any of the building names start with an O? No, not that she could remember. I asked my spirit guides the question again, and I got another O. There was absolutely no other information coming, so I turned to my intuition for help, which I often do when interpreting pictures. I asked my intuition if the O was significant. The response was yes. Thinking that perhaps O meant zero, or that nothing she'd seen so far was right, I asked my intuition if the building she was supposed to rent was among the buildings she had looked at. Again I felt a yes response, so that was not the answer.

Since my client and I were both stuck and unable to interpret the O, I dropped it and moved on to other questions she wanted me to address. After getting clear answers for all of those, I went back to the

O and asked again what it meant. A thought (clairaudience) came into my head that said, "Full circle." I asked my intuition if this meant she was supposed to go back to the original building she had looked at, and it gave me a strong nudge of yes. When I said this to my client, she told me that she had looked at that space several times, and she was hoping that we would confirm that she was on the right track!

I've never met a true psychic who wasn't conscientious about accuracy. No one wants to give misleading information, not to mention the fact that the psychic's reputation is at stake. No one's going to come back to a psychic who repeatedly misdiagnoses information. I know there have been times when I unintentionally gave a client misinformation simply because I misinterpreted what I was seeing.

How These Gifts Work Together

Here's an example that shows how all the psychic gifts work in unison with each other. Currently, there are two popular television shows that are hosted by very gifted psychic mediums, John Edward's *Crossing Over* and *Beyond* with James Van Praagh. Both of these men are excellent examples of how psychic abilities work together. For those of you who have never seen these shows, I'll describe how these abilities work together.

A TV psychic begins by standing in the middle of the set and waits for a strong pull (clairsentience). This pull would feel like there was an energy that suddenly ran from the psychic to the person meant to get the reading on the left side of the room. The psychic would turn in that direction to feel the connection stronger, perhaps getting an image of a male energy (clairvoyance). He or she might see the word "brother," which is clairvoyance, or the feeling of brother might come (clairsentience). Then the psychic might get a picture of an elm tree, along with an image of a mallard duck (clairvoyance). Then the name "Don" might come in as a thought (clairaudience).

If the psychic were in a private session and not on TV, he or she would have time to wait for more pictures to come and possibly put the whole message together by him- or herself. But because this is television, the producers don't want any dead-air time, so the psychic has to move quickly. Once the psychic has an adequate amount of information, he or she will start asking questions, saying something like, "I'm feeling a connection to someone on the left side of the audience. I'm feeling a brother. Who has a deceased brother with a connection to an elm tree? I'm also seeing a mallard duck. The name Don is coming to me. There's a significance to the color yellow. Does any of this mean anything to someone on the left side of the audience?"

At this point, the psychic may not know if the name Don is the deceased person or the person in the audience. As he or she waits for someone in the audience to respond, the psychic is also waiting for the deceased loved one to give more information. At the same time, the psychic knows the producers are watching the clock and also that there are other deceased loved ones waiting to get their turn to speak. In the space of thirty seconds or a minute, the psychic must interpret all the information as accurately as possible. Usually it doesn't take long before someone in the audience responds. For instance, a woman wearing a yellow blouse might raise her hand and say she has a deceased brother named Don who collected replicas of mallard ducks. The psychic, not wanting to make a mistake, will ask what might be significant about an elm tree, and the woman might say, "We lived on Elm Street." Now that the psychic knows who the message is for, he or she would go back to the deceased person to see if there is a specific message for this person. Once he or she has passed this on, or if there isn't a message, the psychic would then step back, clear the deceased person's energy, and ask for the next spirit to move forward.

As a clairvoyant who has struggled with this many times, I would love it if the information came in like a telegram. "Hello, my name is Don. My sister, Velma, is sitting on the left side of the audience in a yellow blouse. We used to live on Elm Street, and when I was living I collected mallard ducks. Please tell my sister I'm doing great, as are Mom and Dad, who are both with me. Tell her we love her." But that isn't how it comes in. Instead, the information arrives in shorthand: brother, sister, yellow, elm, ducks, happy.

I think the only way we're going to make the shift away from thinking of psychics as entertaining fortune tellers is by learning how these gifts work. My repeat clients see their readings with me as a partnership. We work together to unravel some of the goofy pictures I receive so that they can get all the information they need in order to move forward in their lives. They are not looking to be entertained or to have me prove that psychic gifts actually work. They have gotten to the stage where they want to work together with me to solve problems or heal themselves. And I really believe that's how it's supposed to be. Now let's take a look at psychics and what they're all about.

Chapter 2

Professional Psychics

Society's attitude about psychics has changed considerably over the course of history, and I've definitely seen a big shift just in the last thirty-five years. We no longer have to meet in secret. We are not being burned at the stake. Hollywood's portrayal of the psychically gifted has evolved and become more realistic. I can rent space at our local community center to teach my psychic development classes and actually tell the landlord what the classes are about instead of making up some illusive title.

This is the good news, that there is definitely more acceptance of these gifts, but we still have a ways to go. I always tell my students that part of our job as psychics is to break down the stereotypes. Just as everybody possesses some psychic ability, professional psychics are no different from anybody else.

Contrary to popular belief, psychics are not all dark haired, dark eyed, scarf wearing, earring dangling, black cat owners who read people's minds, know when everyone's going to die, and scam people every chance they get. The majority of truly gifted psychics that I have met are hard-working, loving people. Most have a sense of humility about their gifts because they know the gifts come from God, and they therefore take the responsibility that goes along with these gifts seriously. It's been my experience that the majority of truly gifted psychics fight their abilities at first and go through a process of surrendering to them. Of all the well-known psychics today, not one of them grew up hoping to be a psychic.

Psychically gifted people are here to learn and grow and live their lives like everyone else. We're moms and dads, brothers and sisters, sons and daughters. We work hard, struggle with bills, and help our kids with their homework. Many attend church or synagogue. We have hobbies and pets (and not all of them are black cats!). We shop at the mall, bake cookies, mow the grass, do volunteer work, and try to evolve as human beings like everyone else. Simply put, we're regular folks who are always in the process of learning about our gifts and how to work with them.

It's also important to remember that not all psychics are the same. Our gifts and strengths are different. People often *assume* I can contact their deceased relatives like John Edward or James Van Praagh, but I can't do what they do. That isn't how it works.

Psychics often specialize in a certain area. Some are very good at communicating with the deceased (and are called "mediums"). Others, like my brother Michael, are very good with finance and the stock market, and they do readings that focus on business. Some focus on past lives, while others focus completely on the future. There are psychically gifted people whose gift is seeing health challenges inside a body (they are often called "medical intuitives"). Some psychics are able to see and hear ghosts and help them over to the other side (and call themselves "paranormal investigators" or "ghostbusters"). Others can see and read a person's aura, which is the energy field around our body. Some psychics are able to do many of these things, and others express their gifts in only one or two ways. My specialties are working with a person's soul and helping people understand their reasons for being here. I see past lives clearly. I'm able to read sick bodies, and I see and hear ghosts clearly and can help them over to the other side.

When I was taking my psychic development class, I remember our teacher telling us that we each have our own unique way of expressing our gifts. She warned us not to compare ourselves to each other in class because it would only distract us from finding our own true gifts. She told us to find what works best for us and work on strengthening that ability, and that is what most of the professional psychics that I know have done.

Stereotypes

For an example of what life can still be like for a psychic today, see the Sam Raimi movie *The Gift,* which stars Cate Blanchett. The film accurately depicts the common fears and judgments society has about psychically gifted people, and it provides a good taste of how ridiculous the fundamentalist Christians can get. In the final courtroom scene, the prosecuting attorney cross-examines Blanchett with questions that are stereotypical of what people think of psychics, and Blanchett's reaction is, unfortunately, also typical of how defensive psychics can sometimes get.

Thankfully, this is changing as well-known psychics educate the public about themselves and their gifts, and I've included the firsthand, personal stories of five psychically gifted people at the end of this book. On my website (www.echobodine.com), I recommend these five psychics. They graciously agreed to answer a few questions and share a little bit about themselves so that you could gain a better understanding of psychics — their lives, their gifts, and their similarities and differences.

1-800 Hotlines

For millions of people, their only exposure to psychics is the 1-800 psychic hotlines on late-night TV. Until she got busted for fraudulent advertising, Miss Cleo was a staple for late-night watchers, in her colorful turbans and big hoop earrings, proclaiming the great predictions she could make for our lives.

For years, psychic hotlines have been an easy punchline for stand-up comedians, with the joke always being that the psychics who work the phones are all frauds. In 1994 I had the opportunity to attend a private party at Planet Hollywood in Minneapolis for Dionne Warwick and some of the psychics who staff her hotline. They were going from city to city to promote their show, and the Mall of America in Minneapolis was one of their stops. I took my secretary with me, and we were both pleasantly surprised with the two psychics who gave us readings. They knew nothing about us, other than that we were sitting at the head table with Dionne. The psychic who worked with me, Robert from New York, said that he wanted to read me because I was sitting with "the boss." He didn't ask for my name or anything else about me. He just dove in and gave me information about my career, the book I was writing, my finances, and my love life. He was amazingly accurate, and my secretary had the same experience with the psychic who read her.

Were all the psychics on her hotline just as good? I have no idea. Are all the late-night TV psychics for real? I wish I could tell you that all the psychics you see on television come from a place of integrity and that you can trust them, but I can't say that. Every profession has scam artists and I have no idea what the ratio would be on these hotlines. I asked Robert why he chose to work for the psychic network rather than go out on his own, and he said he didn't want the hassle of marketing himself. He also said he liked the people who worked there, and it was a great company to be involved with.

Shortly after Dionne Warwick's event, I met a young woman who worked on another psychic network. She had no idea who I was or what I did for a living. I asked her how she got her psychic information, and she said that she made up stuff as she went along. When I asked her if she had any psychic abilities, she looked at me like she had no idea what I was talking about and replied, "Hey, whatever pays the bills." I stood there dumbfounded. I didn't bother to give her my speech on honesty and integrity among psychics because clearly she couldn't have cared less. Shortly after this encounter, I heard that the woman was no longer employed at the hotline, and I was glad to hear it.

I hate it when people in my profession don't come from a place of integrity, but it's not realistic to think that all will. There are scam artists in every profession. There is nothing inherent in having psychic abilities that makes people behave honestly or dishonestly. But again, just as in any profession, a few high-profile frauds can easily taint all psychics with a bad rap.

How to Spot Scam Artists

The first thing to keep in mind is that scam artists, whatever their supposed profession, are in it for the money. Many years ago, someone came up to my dad at a concert and told him that she could see dark clouds in his aura that meant he had danger ahead, but for a mere five thousand dollars the person could clear this awful curse and protect him from harm. Fortunately, my dad refused, though he did call me as soon as he got home to ask if something like this was possible. I told him it was total garbage and not to give it another thought. But there are many people out there who don't know who to call or contact when they receive "bad news" via one of these so-called psychics.

As I was working on this chapter, a woman sent me four different letters she had received in the mail from various people claiming to be psychics. Each letter forecast some kind of doom and gloom and asked for a fee so that the writer could help her get rid of this negative thing happening in her life. One letter talked about a curse that had been put on her: "This is your last chance. In the next twenty-four hours, the curse must be broken and your miracles must begin."

Another letter said that she was this woman's "dream psychic" and that they had met the previous night in the woman's dream. The letter went on and on about various negative symbols in the woman's dreams and what she must do to ward off this negativity, which included sending the dream psychic twenty-five dollars in order to perform the "Dream Ritual of the Archangel Gabriel." Another letter went on for four pages telling this woman about the negative things that would happen to her on specific dates *if* she didn't send Madame twenty-five dollars. The last letter was equally pathetic, except this psychic wanted double the price, fifty dollars, to remove "the black cloud circling her aura."

These prices may seem small, but believe me, they are only the beginning. Once these scam artists know they've got someone terrified of black clouds, or curses, or whatever, they will keep asking for more and more money. I've heard stories of people who eventually paid thousands of dollars to so-called psychics to protect them from evil events. These situations are all so incredibly sad, whenever and however they occur, but they have nothing to do with true psychic gifts. Scam artists will always try to scare you and then claim they are the only ones who can help — and for a fee. These are the people to watch out for.

If you are currently shopping for a psychic, here are some very simple tips:

- If possible, only go to someone you've been referred to by a good friend.

- Whenever you're thinking about going to a psychic, or interviewing one, check your intuition: Is this the right time for you to do it? Is this is the right person? Trust your response.

- If you're going through a painful, vulnerable time — such as losing a loved one through death or divorce, finding out you have a serious health problem, losing your job, finding out your kid is on drugs, and so on — don't rush to the first psychic you can find. When times are tough, it's natural to want to know how certain situations are going to turn out, but when we're feeling desperate, we're also vulnerable, and that's what scam artists count on. If you feel panicked, give yourself time to calm your fears, and then ask around for a reputable psychic who can help you get through the situation. You don't need to be victimized twice.

Discerning Who's Who

There's a very good section in the Bible, Matthew 7:15–20, about how to discern between a false prophet and the real deal that I believe applies to all professions: "Beware of false prophets who come disguised as harmless sheep, but are really wolves that will tear you apart. You can detect them by the way they act, just as you can identify a tree by its fruit. You don't pick grapes from thornbushes, or figs from thistles. A healthy tree produces good fruit, and an unhealthy tree produces bad fruit. A good tree can't produce bad fruit, and a bad tree can't produce good fruit. So every tree that does not produce good fruit is chopped down and thrown into the fire. Yes, the way to identify a tree or a person is by the kind of fruit that is produced."

If a person who has psychic abilities is good and honorable and comes from a place of integrity, he or she won't need to advertise. Word of mouth will spread, and the person will have all the work he or she can handle. The person will produce good fruit. If a person is not psychically gifted but is claiming to be, he or she will not produce good fruit and his or her business will not flourish. It's as simple as that.

Misconceptions about Psychics and Their Abilities

A friend of mine was staying at a hotel in Chicago that offered psychic readings during Happy Hour, so she thought she'd check it out. When she sat down, the psychic asked her if she wanted her handwriting analyzed, a card reading (using a regular deck of playing cards), or her palm read. My friend decided to go with the cards, and later said the reading was "interesting." One of the most common misconceptions about psychics is that these kinds of "readings" are typical of psychics but please note that none of these tools has any direct relationship with true psychic gifts.

Even within my profession there can be confusion over the term "psychic." Over the past thirty-five years I've worked with psychics, attended conferences and psychic fairs, trained psychic people, and gone to numerous psychics to see how others work, and I've learned that not everyone who claims to be a psychic is actually gifted psychically. True psychics are people who use clairvoyance, clairaudience, and/or clairsentience when they give a reading. They don't need cards, tarot or otherwise. They don't need to know your birthdate (that's astrology). They don't need to read rune stones or the *I Ching*. They don't need a sample of your handwriting. They don't need to consult a Ouija board or look at your palm. A true psychic needs no other tools than their God-given gifts. Though some professional psychics will use these tools as aids in their work, they rely first and foremost on their gifts.

Many people who have not developed their psychic abilities will call themselves "psychics" because they have learned to use these tools. However, they are relying on these tools completely for information. I prefer to call these people, and not disparagingly, fortune tellers, since they are telling your future based on what the cards, the stones, or the board has to say. I always tell my students the first night of class that if they want to use any of these tools, I prefer that they wait until after they've completed the course and have developed their abilities *first*. Then if they want to use any of these aids in their work, they can.

Indeed, psychic information is not always easy to interpret, and these tools can help clarify the messages we receive. For example, let's say a man goes to a clairvoyant to find out why he hasn't met Ms. Right, and the clairvoyant gets a picture in her third eye of a cave. Her job is to interpret the meaning of that image accurately. If she's learned how to work with her gift of sight, she'll enlist the help of her intuition and consider various interpretations to see which one gets a positive response. She might ask her intuition, Does the cave symbolize an unsociable person? *Sort of.* Loner? *Getting closer.* Not much communication with the outside world? *Almost there.* Is this person shy, stays home most of the time, and doesn't make himself available to the opposite sex? *Bingo!* That's the correct answer. The intuition will give a strong nudge of yes when the clairvoyant gets the right interpretation.

Now let's say that same person asks a tarot card reader why he hasn't met Ms. Right, and the tarot card reader will probably draw the Hermit card in this particular situation. The definition for this card varies with different tarot decks, but the basic interpretation is that the person spends a lot of time in seclusion. The cards can be helpful when interpreting the pictures in a general way, but if the reader isn't psychic, then the answers the cards provide will be limited.

Misconceptions

The end of year was fast approaching, and I got a call from a reporter who said he was writing an article called "Getting a Psychic Reading for the New Year." He wanted some general information, such as prices and what people could expect for their money. I was a little taken aback by the focus of his article, which presented this as a fun idea, and asked him if he had ever been to a psychic for a reading. He hadn't, so I explained that getting a reading for the new year might not necessarily be a positive experience because there are so many things that could go on in a person's life, good and bad, and you might not want to know about them all. In fact, years ago a friend of mine asked me on New Year's Eve if I would take a psychic look at what the next year had in store for him. The first image that came to me was of several dark clouds. Then I saw his sister in the hospital with both legs in casts, his brother confined to a wheelchair, his mother having a stroke, and my friend attending someone's funeral. My guides said he would spend most of the year taking care of other people. I remember wishing that he hadn't asked me for a reading, and I tried to give him the information as gently as I could so as not to overwhelm him. This experience certainly was a good lesson for both of us as far as not looking at psychic readings as a form of entertainment.

Several months after the reading, I ran into my friend at the funeral of one of our mutual friends, and he told me that all four predictions had come true. He said when I first gave him the information, he wished he hadn't asked, but that looking back, he was glad he was mentally prepared for each thing as it happened.

The reporter and I ended up spending almost an hour on the phone talking about psychics and the false assumptions people make about us. Even people who have experience with psychics sometimes hold onto these misconceptions, which are perpetuated by movies, horror stories, religion, and popular culture. Here is a list of the most common misconceptions:

We are psychically tuned into people and world events 24/7.

As far as being tuned into world events twenty-four hours a day, seven days a week, this is a fallacy. Psychics don't know what is happening twenty-four hours a day, seven days a week. This isn't to say we don't feel certain things. Many psychics can sense natural disasters approaching, and many psychics felt that something bad was going to happen around the date of the 9/11 terrorist attacks in the United States. However, to my knowledge, no psychics were able to pinpoint what exactly was going to occur or where. In any case, tuning into world events on a daily basis would be such an energy drain that I can't imagine doing it. Most professional psychics that I know protect themselves from feeling these events because, as we've learned the hard way, there's nothing we can do about them anyway. Most professional psychics take a break from their work just like everyone else. Most of us make sure our abilities are "shut off" when we're out in public, so that we don't pick up information from or about people. (How to do this will be described in chapter 6.)

Psychics read people's minds.

This is such an interesting one because on the one hand, the answer is no, we can't intentionally read people's minds. However, this is an interesting question because psychics who are gifted with clairaudience often unknowingly pick up thoughts from other people — what we call mental telepathy. It's been my experience that when I am picking up on the thoughts of someone around me I'm usually not aware that they are someone else's thoughts. Only recently have I begun deliberately experimenting with mental telepathy to see if I can tell the difference, in my own head, between my random thoughts and the thoughts of other people around me. While this is not easy, I am slowly learning how to discern between the two. Can we intentionally read people's minds? No. Can we pick up on their thoughts? Yes.

Psychics see people's deep, dark secrets.

This answer is similar to the last one. We can't intentionally see people's secrets but if a person is thinking very hard about a secret they're hoping we can't see, a psychic may pick up on it simply because the thoughts are out there. Another way of looking at this is that we don't randomly pick up on people's deep dark secrets unless they want us to.

Psychics automatically know when and how people are going to die.

This is one of those "I wish I had a dollar for every time someone asked me" questions. The answer, plain and simple, is no. Psychics aren't privy to the information on how or when a person is going to die because it is not an easy one to predict. The few times that I have seen someone's death *before* it occurs, I was given the information by the person's soul with strict instructions not to share the information with the person. (You can read more about this in my book *Echoes of the Soul*.)

Psychics can see their own futures.

Whenever anything out of the ordinary happens in my life, someone usually asks me how come I didn't know it was going to happen, but one of the ironic truths of being psychic is that the hardest person to read is yourself. While it is possible for a psychic to read his or her own future, it is difficult because, in order to clearly interpret the information you receive, you need to be emotionally detached from any of the information. This may sound obvious, but when it comes to your own life, it's almost impossible to remain detached. The even greater irony is that once a psychic (or anyone, for that matter) reaches that level of emotional detachment, he or she can see a great deal about his or her life and future, but once you've become that detached, you've reached the point where you usually don't care what's coming. Your attitude is simply that you take the good with the bad whenever it arrives.

Psychics who do want psychic information about their own lives usually go to other psychics, or if they are able to detach emotionally, they get their information in meditation.

Psychics know the winning lottery numbers.

Once again, this is one of those instances where we would need to be completely detached in order to get accurate lottery numbers, and usually if you're playing the lottery, you're playing to win and aren't emotionally detached.

Psychics are all on a spiritual path.

This is a misconception I had for many years. Because I believe psychic gifts come from God and that it is important to be on a spiritual path, I assumed all psychics believed this. However, I've since met a few psychically gifted people who don't share my beliefs or follow a spiritual path. We are as varied as people everywhere, and our individual beliefs have less to do with our gifts than with the beliefs we were raised with, our life experiences, and the level our soul has progressed to.

All psychics work alike.

We are similar in how we work, but we each have our own way of expressing our abilities.

All psychics read palms.

Reading palms is not an automatic part of being psychic. If someone reads palms, they have taken a class or learned it from a book.

Psychics only see good things.

If this were only true, my work would be so much easier, but it's not. We see the good as well as the bad, as my friend discovered when he asked for that New Year's Eve reading.

Psychics know where all the missing children are.

This one is a heartbreaker. I sure wish we could find all the children, pets, and adults who are missing — as well as their captors — but this can be very difficult to do. It really is like finding a needle in a haystack. As I explained earlier, psychic information doesn't arrive like a telegram, with all the details spelled out. Psychics can see or sense if a person is alive or dead. They can get pictures of wooded areas or bodies of water. But it is very difficult to accurately pinpoint an *exact* location. In addition, the more emotionally involved the psychic is, the more difficult it will be, since the psychic might block out pertinent information because he or she might not want to see the *truth* of the situation. (We will explore this further in chapter 4.)

Psychic abilities and intuition are the same thing.

Psychic abilities and intuition are not the same thing. Even the location of these two are different. Clairvoyance and clairaudience are located in our head; clairsentience is a sensing in the body; and intuition is our inner knowing located in our solar plexus, heart, or gut area, depending upon the person. (This difference is addressed further in chapter 5.)

Psychic abilities are evil.

Only intentions can be evil, not psychic abilities themselves. Psychic abilities are similar to our other five senses: they are a way to receive information. What we do with that information is up to us. This question is most often asked by people who are devoutly religious, and I address what the Bible has to say about psychic abilities in chapter 3.

Psychic readings are written in stone.

Always remember that psychics can misinterpret the information they receive and the timing of the prediction can be off. It's also important to evaluate every psychic reading using your own intuition, which will let you know if the information is accurate or not. In addition, psychic predictions don't eliminate free will; your actions can make a difference. Just because a psychic makes a prediction doesn't mean it will necessarily come true. (I will talk more about this in chapter 5.)

Psychics can get very detailed information.

I can't tell you the number of women who have asked if I could give them the name, address and phone number of their husband's mistress. We don't receive information like that. As confusing as this sounds, we get general information that is specific. We might get a physical description, a first name, and the town the woman lives in, but not the minute details that people think we can (like the specific cave Bin Laden is hiding in).

Psychics on television represent all psychics.

Nowadays, when anyone mentions the word *psychic,* people automatically think of the high-profile ones on TV, such as James Van Praagh on *Beyond,* John Edward on *Crossing Over,* or Sylvia Browne. People have come to assume that all psychics are just like the ones on television, but it just isn't so. We are as different as any other random group of people. TV producers make a living by creating entertaining programs, so in addition to selecting psychics who are accurate and fast, they want ones who are also attractive, polished, funny, charming, and not intimidated by cameras or crowds. The majority of psychics I know are actually introverts — they would rather have a root canal than do their work in front of cameras knowing that millions of people are watching. Most psychics prefer to read their clients in the privacy of their home or office because they know the information that comes through is often very personal. They also want to do their work without any particular time limits because producers hate dead-air time or the feeling that they have to "perform."

One attribute I think is important for TV psychics to have is a thick skin. By becoming a public personality, you also become a target of debunkers and others who have no respect for the profession. Most psychics I know are pretty sensitive and would not be eager to become a lightning rod for criticism. In the end, I would say it's the rare person who has all the attributes necessary to be successful on a TV program.

Chapter 3

What the Bible Says about Psychic Abilities

When I first got the vision for this book and specifically this chapter, I set out on a journey determined to find everything the Bible has to say about psychic abilities. I went through that book with a fine-toothed comb, read other books about the Bible, and watched several videos on biblical times. I really wanted to make sure I had done a thorough job and by the end of that year, I compiled a forty-page chapter on everything the Bible has to say about psychics and this gift. I tediously typed up any scripture that made reference to prophets, seers, fortune tellers, diviners, or enchanters and then quoted several verses from the Old and the New Testament. I was determined to show all my readers who are struggling with their psychic gifts that they are not going against their religion by developing their abilities.

My publisher at New World Library, Marc Allen, has a rule of thumb that he *suggests* to his authors before turning in a manuscript. Go over every sentence to see if you could say it better and shorter and then go over it again doing the same thing. Then when you think it's ready to be turned in, go over it one more time.

I wanted to include as much as possible because, after all, I was on a mission to set the record straight. It was tough to be objective and whittle it down but I did manage to cut out about ten pages of scripture and I proudly turned in my thirty-page chapter. For those of you who don't know Marc Allen, he's a very gentle man, who has a *way* of convincing an author that they need to whittle some more without actually coming right out and saying, "Forty pages of Bible quotes? Are you crazy?" So when Marc called and said, "Echo, we need to talk about the religion chapter," I knew it was whittling time. Besides wanting me to cut it down quite a bit, he also pointed out that the way I was presenting the information wasn't my usual style of informal, friendly, and informative. He said that I sounded more like I was standing in front of a class giving a boring lecture on Bible statistics and quotes and he was right. I was so determined to present as much information as I could that I went totally into my head and wrote it from a very mental, "here's all the facts" point of view.

After my whittling conversation with Marc, I walked away from the project for about a month. I needed to clear my head, get back to my usual writing style, and keep it simple. I went back to the drawing board and decided to rewrite the entire chapter.

Before I get into the Bible, I'd like to tell you why this chapter is so important to me.

Throughout my life as a psychic, I've had more than my share of fundamentalist Christians tell me that according to the Bible the work I do is evil, I work for Satan, and I'm going straight to hell. I've had death threats, lost friends, and received hateful, anonymous letters quoting scripture from the Old Testament, with many claiming to take on my salvation as their personal challenge.

I've gathered the following information on the Bible, however, not so much to counter narrow-minded religious fanatics as to reassure Christian readers that they aren't going against their religion by developing their psychic abilities. I am a Christian, and I have struggled with the question of whether my abilities and my faith were incompatible, and I've seen many of my students engaged in this same struggle. In fact, one of my students recently told me that she went to her minister to tell him that she was taking psychic development classes because she's had prophetic dreams and visions since she was a little girl. The minister told her to stop taking these classes immediately because she was only going to attract evil to her. She came to me in tears wondering what she should do. Her religion was, and is, an important part of her life, and she felt as if her minister were making her choose between the two.

There's no need to choose. The Bible itself does not support the idea that psychic abilities are evil. I may not be a biblical scholar, but I want to do a thorough job, and I really want to understand, as much as we can know today, what the Bible actually says about psychic abilities and what people believed over two thousand years ago.

The Bible

One thing I've come to learn is that the Bible itself, in the form we have it today, is not a perfect record of the events and times it contains. This is not to say that the Bible is wrong, or that we can simply ignore the parts we don't like. What I mean is that the Bible we read in church every Sunday is a translation several times over, and even the New Testament prophets were writing fifty to seventy years after the events they describe. Just like the children's game of Telephone — where children sit in a circle and pass around a spoken message in secret only to find that, by the time it reaches the last person, the message has been significantly changed — we can't know with certainty that everything we read is actually as it was said or even done.

For instance, it's important to remember that the original scriptures that became the Old Testament were written in Hebrew, which were then translated into Greek and then Latin, which is the language that the first English translation is based on. Much of the New Testament was written in Greek, and then translated into Latin, and then English and other languages. When the English priest William Tyndale (1494–1536) created this first English translation in the sixteenth century, he was accused of perverting the scriptures and forced to leave England. His New Testament was burned as "untrue translations." In 1536, he was executed by strangling and then burned at the stake. Eventually, the church reversed its opinion, and William Tyndale is now honored as the "Father of the English Bible."

The King James Version was first produced in 1611, and over the centuries, it has been revised several times. The Revised Standard Version, published in 1952, remains the most popular translation, while the New Revised Standard Version was published in 1989, and other versions are being developed every year. Currently, there are over three thousand versions of the Bible, and over two hundred denominations within Christianity.

The Old Testament

By my count, the Old Testament contains close to five hundred references to seers and prophets (at one time, prophets were referred to as seers), and the majority of them are positive. In fact, eighteen of the thirty-nine books in the Old Testament are messages from or about Hebrew prophets. And as described in the Old Testament, the abilities of the prophets — the ability to see visions, hear voices, and sense spirits and God — are exactly the same abilities of clairvoyance, clairaudience, and clairsentience. Something I find interesting is that in Old Testament times priests and prophets usually hung out together, and often when God was mad at one of them, he was mad at the other. I also found several scriptures that warn people about discerning false prophets from true prophets. See Lamentations 2:14, Lamentations 2:20, Lamentations 4:13, Ezekiel 13:2–4, Ezekiel 13:9–10, Ezekiel 13:17–23, Ezekiel 14:9–10, Hoseah 4:4–6, Micah 3:5–7, Micah 3:11, Zephaniah 3:4, and Zechariah 13:2–5.

One thing the Old Testament makes very clear is that prophets and fortune tellers are *not* the same thing. Prophets were considered to be messengers of God, whereas fortune tellers were clumped in the same category as sorcerers, diviners, enchanters, and witchcraft. See Leviticus 19:26, Leviticus 19:31, Leviticus 20:6, and Deuteronomy 18:10–14.

These scriptures make perfect sense to me, and none of it says that what I do for people is wrong. Don't turn to fortune tellers. Turn to God. Don't get distracted by sorcerers or enchanters. Don't get involved in black magic and hurt others.

The Bible makes it clear that we should turn to God in times of need. I've seen so many "New Age junkies" who have no idea what spirituality is all about. They go from psychic to psychic hoping to be entertained and distracted from their own lives. I've seen people who have lost loved ones become so obsessed with communicating with them after death that they forget to live their lives. In both these cases, psychic abilities are not at fault, but the purposes that people put them to become unhealthy and even self-destructive. The message in the scriptures is the same. They simply warn people to turn to God and not get distracted by those who would lead them away, such as scam artists and magic charmers. This advice is just as applicable for today.

The New Testament

The New Testament mainly describes the ministry and death of Jesus, who was a Hebrew rabbi named Jeshua ben Joseph (Teacher Jesus son of Joseph). After Jesus' crucifixion, the New Testament describes the acts of his disciples (or apostles) and the beginnings of Christianity.

During his era, Jeshua was considered a radical teacher, healer, and prophet. He taught the Jews and Gentiles that God was a loving God, and that they could talk to him directly without having to go to priests and prophets. In essence, he taught spiritual principles and broke the laws of the Old Testament when he felt they weren't necessary or had become a distraction from worshiping God and doing his works, such as when he would heal on the Sabbath even though the priests insisted it must be a day of rest.

As Ken Davis says in *Don't Know Much about the Bible* about our modern age: "The Bible was composed a long time ago for a very different group of people than we are today. People have to determine what laws are appropriate to desert nomads four thousand years ago, and which are universal laws that transcend time." This is exactly what Jesus did in his ministry, by interpreting the Old Testament for the people of his time.

Jesus performed miracles, healed the sick, and raised the dead. He taught the crowds by telling stories and parables. He came to teach us how to live our lives and to show us our potential as children of God. Jesus had visions (clairvoyance), he *knew* what others were thinking (clairaudience), and he *knew* how people felt (clairsentience). He taught his disciples how to prophesy and heal, and he said, "These gifts I give unto you and greater works shall you do" (John 14:12).

Before his crucifixion, he told his disciples that God was going to send another comforter (or counselor) who would never leave us, and that is the Holy Spirit (John 14:16). According to the Bible, after the death of Jesus, a young Pharisee named Saul had been given the authority to arrest the followers of Jesus. On his way to Damascus, Saul had a spiritual awakening that changed his life forever. First, he was visited by Jesus, who asked him why he was persecuting him. Saul then went blind for three days, until he was healed by Ananias (Acts 9:17). In order to reflect and embody this life-changing experience, Saul changed his name to Paul, and he began spreading the teachings of Jesus. He traveled extensively and started many churches. He was an educated man, and he wrote letters and instructions to the various churches he started, and some of these letters are now part of the Bible. Even though Jesus said Simon Peter was the man who would build his church, Paul was without a doubt one of the main figures who began Christianity.

In Paul's letters to the Corinthians, he talks about the "Gifts of the Spirit," and this is where we clearly see that the counselor that Jesus referred to (the Holy Spirit) has given all of us the Gift of Prophecy (1 Corinthians 12): "And now, dear brothers and sisters, I will write about the special abilities the Holy Spirit gives to each of us, for I must correct your misunderstandings about them."

1 Corinthians 12:8–11: "To one person the Spirit gives the ability to give wise advice; to another he gives the gift of special knowledge. He gives special faith to another and to some else the power to heal the sick. He gives one person the power to perform miracles, and to another the ability to prophesy. He gives someone else the ability to know whether it is really the Spirit of God or another spirit that is speaking. Still another person is given the ability to speak in unknown languages and another is given the ability to interpret what is being

said. It is the one and only Holy Spirit who distributes these gifts. He alone decides which gift each person should have."

1 Corinthians 14:1: "Let love be your highest goal, but also desire the special abilities the Spirit gives, especially the gift of prophecy."

1 Corinthians 14:3: "But one who prophesies is helping others grow in the Lord, encouraging and comforting them."

1 Corinthians 14:5: "I wish you all had the gift of speaking in tongues, but even more I wish you were all able to prophesy. For prophecy is a greater and more useful gift than speaking in tongues."

1 Corinthians 14:22: "So you see that speaking in tongues is a sign, not for believers, but for unbelievers; prophecy, however, is for the benefit of believers, not unbelievers."

1 Corinthians 12:27–28: "Now all of you together are Christ's body, and each one of you is a separate and necessary part of it. Here is a list of some of the members that God has placed in the body of Christ: first are apostles, second are prophets, third are teachers, then those who do miracles, those who have the gift of healing, those who can help others, those who speak in unknown languages."

It should be noted that nowhere in Corinthians are the words "evil" or "Satan" ever mentioned when Paul is describing the Gifts of the Spirit, and he clearly points out that the Gift of Prophecy (which is the result of psychic abilities) comes from the Holy Spirit.

This next quote, not written by Paul but from Acts, is important because it refutes another thing many fundamentalists believe — that only certain people can prophesy:

Acts 2:17–18: "In the last days, God said, I will pour out my Spirit upon all people. Your sons and daughters will prophesy, your young men will see visions, and your old men will dream dreams. In those days I will pour out my Spirit upon all my servants, men and women alike, and they will prophesy."

Given the evidence in the Bible, it shouldn't be a surprise, then, that Jesus would appear to me on Easter morning to say that psychic abilities are gifts from God and that our religious leaders should be developing their own psychic abilities and then teaching them in their churches and synagogues. I'd say we're a long way from that happening, but I hold out hope that someday our religious leaders will stop disparaging psychic abilities and acknowledge them as special gifts from the Holy Spirit.

I have no idea how long that is going to take. I am frequently reminded, though, of something Jesus said to narrow-minded religious leaders in his own time: "How terrible it will be for you experts in religious law! For you hide the key to knowledge from the people. You don't enter the Kingdom yourselves, and you prevent others from entering" (Luke 11:52).

In Closing

I have no idea how long it's going to take for religion to honor these gifts. Jim Marion, who studied for the Catholic priesthood, wrote an intense and highly recommended book called *Putting on the Mind of Christ:* "As long as modern-day Christianity does not accept prophetic messages from modern-day prophets, they are missing out on a great deal of wise information coming through to us today." I couldn't agree with him more.

I believe if we just keep moving forward, asking God to guide us with our Gifts of the Spirit, we'll know what to do. We can't let the prejudices and negative opinions of others slow us down. I am so grateful I didn't cave in years ago when certain friends of mine asked me to give up my gifts. I'm so grateful I've continued to live by the voice within rather than the negative, fearful voices outside of me. In the end, it all boils down to a simple question: Are we acting on faith or fear? Are we listening to God or the world? Are we being true to ourselves or true to others?

And Greater Works Shall You Do

In a recent conversation with James Van Praagh, he was telling me about an experience he had with a gifted psychic and ghostbuster he met in Oklahoma: not only did the woman identify three ghosts by their full names and discover the reasons the spirits were earthbound, but she also led him to the correct cemetery and the exact gravesites where the ghosts' bodies were buried!

When James told me about this, my first thought was amazement, which was quickly followed by my second thought, skepticism. My rational mind raced to explain how this woman could get this kind of detailed information about a ghost's grave. I didn't think it was possible, and I thought maybe she had driven to this particular cemetery before she met with James and picked out three different people who were buried there. Then when she and James did their ghostbusting job, she simply told James that the three ghosts were named such and such and that she had a vision of where they were buried.

Such a good, logical explanation satisfied the skeptic in me, but there was the other side, the psychic side, that wanted to know if this was really possible. Then it occurred to me: the only reason I was doubting the woman's abilities was simply because I had never seen anyone do this before.

The same thing happened the first time I ever saw James Van Praagh on television communicating with the dead. My logical mind was going crazy trying to figure out how he could bring through such detailed information. I had never seen it done before, so I didn't know that that kind of expression of psychic abilities was possible. Then John Edward appeared on the scene and boggled my mind again.

I guess it's human nature to doubt the claims any person makes when the rest of us haven't experienced it firsthand. Fortunately, that doesn't stop all the pioneers from discovering new things.

Jesus tells us in John 12:14, "These gifts I give unto you and greater works shall you do." That's powerful stuff. He's telling us that we will do greater works than he did. And in order to do that, we have to open up our minds and stop thinking with limitations. Often in my prayers, I ask God to help me move past my fears and self-doubt so that I can get to the next level psychically, so that I might experience what Jesus meant when he said, "...and greater works shall you do."

The most important thing is to keep learning and to keep teaching what we learn. In recent years, I've been encouraged by psychic television shows, which are slowly moving away from being *only* about entertainment and instead exploring the potential of these gifts. Many of the people who watch shows on the paranormal are experiencing these gifts themselves, and they are looking for guidance and understanding. It's pretty obvious to me when I give a lecture on psychic phenomenon that people are starving for information on the subject.

I'm feeling optimistic that in my lifetime the media will one day respect these abilities as the gifts they truly are and provide us with examples of what's possible. If we didn't see Tiger Woods doing his magic on the golf course or Steven Spielberg demonstrating what's possible in the world of cinematography, we wouldn't believe people could do those things, either.

I believe that one day when we describe someone as psychic the last image that will come to mind will be that of an old, toothless gypsy fortune teller. Someday, we will truly understand the truth about these gifts, and such prejudices will become a part of history. We live in exciting times!

Chapter 4

Psychic Development Preliminaries

You don't have to become a professional psychic who does readings for a living in order to develop your psychic abilities. The pictures, thoughts, and feelings that come to us psychically from God and our guides are primarily meant to help us with whatever life experience we happen to be dealing with. Developing your psychic gifts is a way to improve the way you live your life; it's not necessarily the start of a career.

We all have psychic abilities, just as we all have abilities in music, math, the arts, and so on. There are lots of people who choose not to focus on or develop their psychic gifts, but that doesn't mean the potential isn't always there. Just because up to now a person hasn't felt compelled to develop that part of him- or herself doesn't mean that person can't or won't in the future.

When God created us, God gave us unlimited potential, and our soul's goal is to discover and develop its potential in all areas. Developing this unlimited potential couldn't possibly take place in one lifetime, which is one of the reasons why we continue to reincarnate here on Earth. If you're feeling called to explore your psychic gifts, your soul has either chosen to begin your development in this lifetime or to continue its development from previous lives.

This is why people in the same psychic development class will all be at different levels in their abilities. Some have already begun this journey and their development is going to come quicker and easier, while some are just starting to explore their psychic gifts. They will take longer and question it more.

PSYCHIC JOURNAL

I've had many students who have developed their gifts in previous lives but are blocked in this lifetime because of past-life trauma. In their previous life, they suffered as a result of having these gifts, and their soul is on the fence about whether they want to go further in their development or keep that door closed. As the class progresses, these students might encounter unexpected blocks and difficulties to work through. Something I've found very helpful for anyone hoping to develop their psychic abilities, but especially for those having difficulties, is journaling.

If you are in process of developing your gifts, get a journal that you can reserve specifically for recording all of your thoughts, feelings, fears, blocks, anticipations, expectations, and visions as you progress. Journaling about the different stages of your development will help you sort everything out. If you're feeling blocked or anxious, if old fears crop up, if past-life memories come to the surface regarding these abilities, or if you have nightmares about these abilities, writing them out will help tremendously. Recording mental telepathy experiences will help build your confidence in your clairaudient ability. It's very beneficial to get out all your feelings on paper so that they don't block your progress. Try to journal something about your spiritual path or psychic development every day. You'll enjoy looking back at your growth.

A SPECIAL NOTE TO TEENAGERS

Over the years, many parents have asked me if I would teach a class specifically designed for their teenagers who are displaying psychic abilities, and I've also received numerous requests from teens asking the same thing. My inner voice has always answered with an emphatic *no*. One day in meditation I asked why this isn't a good idea, and my inner voice said that teenagers go through enough changes as it is and that opening up psychically could be too much for them. There is a tremendous responsibility that goes along with being psychic, and many teenagers aren't emotionally mature enough to handle those yet.

To some teenagers, getting or having visions may sound cool, but in reality it is a lot more involved. Psychics receive "negative" information that could overwhelm young hearts, such as pregnant women losing their babies, spouses who are cheating on each other, bankruptcy, someone about to lose his job, a murder or death, cancer or other serious illness inside someone's body, and national or worldwide catastrophes.

Some teenagers want to develop their abilities because they think being psychic will give them power. Others think that it will impress their friends, and others simply want to snoop into other people's lives. None of these are good reasons for developing psychic abilities.

If you are a teenager hoping to develop your psychic abilities now, please consider waiting a few years until you get more experience and wisdom under your belt. Put the whole issue on hold. Once you've become an independent adult, you can return to all of this and explore whether or not you want to do anything with your psychic gifts. I promise you, they won't go away. Don't make your life more complicated than it already is or burden yourself with any added responsibility.

DETACHMENT

Whenever new students tell me they can't wait to develop their abilities so that they can help people, I get concerned because caring too much can actually get in the way of being a good psychic.

There are two kinds of caretakers in the world, and many well-intentioned people don't know the difference. Unhealthy caretakers come from a needy place. They help others in order to feel good about themselves and because they want people to like them. Oftentimes they set up situations where people must rely on them so they will continue to be needed.

Healthy caretakers don't have a personal agenda other than to assist others in whatever they're going through. Healthy caretakers detach their emotions so that they can give the person whatever the person needs. That doesn't mean you can't be loving or caring; it just means keeping your own needs in check and understanding that we can only truly heal ourselves, not others. Healthy caretakers learn to let go of their expectations concerning the outcome of the information they receive.

Psychics, especially, need to learn to become healthy caregivers. Psychics who get into this work to save the world soon develop a "savior complex," and invariably they burn out fast and are ineffective.

In order to be effective, we have to keep ourselves out of the readings when we're doing them. Detachment is very important when giving psychic information. It's tough delivering bad news to people, and there is always the temptation to fudge the truth in order to spare feelings. And yet it's unhealthy to deliver good news if it's not true. I've met psychics who give cheerful, positive readings so that their clients will feel good and keep coming back, but what these psychics fail to realize (though eventually they get it) is that if the information isn't accurate, the clients aren't going to return. More importantly, however, the client will believe and act on this false information, leading to potentially more pain and problems when events don't come to pass as expected.

We are the messengers, the channels that the information comes through. We can deliver that information in a loving, caring way, but we must remember not to get involved in the situations of others in order to help them fix their problems. That's their responsibility.

GIVING ADVICE VERSUS CHANNELING INFORMATION

What do you do if you go to Al-Anon and think it's the greatest thing since sliced bread and a friend of yours asks for some psychic guidance regarding her lousy marriage to her alcoholic husband? Or what if you're a cancer survivor and a client tells you she has cancer and wants to know if she'll get better? What do you do if you're pro-life and a client wants help deciding whether or not to get an abortion? Or — and this one happened to me — what do you do if a client asks for advice on a man she's dating and it turns out to be the same guy you're dating?

Do you tell your friend to go to Al-Anon because you believe in it so much, or tell the person with cancer that of course she'll survive the cancer because you did, or tell the pregnant woman *not* to get an abortion because you don't believe in it, or tell the woman dating your boyfriend not to date the guy anymore, and not because he's two-timing but because he's yours? No, no, no, and no.

Remember, clients are not paying for our opinions! Even if you're reading friends and family, they are interested in the information you are getting, not your advice. That doesn't mean you can't share your personal feelings briefly, but it's important to clarify which information is from the guides and then you can go on to say, "My personal feeling or experience is such and such." Maybe Al-Anon won't be as successful for this person as it was for you, or maybe they won't survive cancer. It is possible that there's an important karmic piece she's working out with the person she's dating and you don't want to interfere. We can't assume that we know what another person needs. You know what they say happens whenever you *assume.*

Our natural instinct is to be helpful and soothing, but always remember that our job, whether we are being paid or not, is to give clear, accurate information in as professional and respectful a manner as possible. This, in itself, is exactly what people want and need in order to accomplish whatever it is that's before them. Each person must follow his or her own unique path. Our only job is to help the person follow that path.

WHERE DOES THE INFORMATION COME FROM?

In the beginning of my psychic development, I never knew who was giving me the information. The Ouija board spelled out grand names such as Zoltar and Unonden, and the voices said they were very high spiritual guides. But the messages weren't congruent with a high master teacher or guide. After initially grabbing my interest, their messages turned toward the negative and the dramatic, such as "So and so is sick and will die soon," or "Your friend John will die in a car accident." Looking back, I now know that these were earthbound spirits, or ghosts, trying to mess with my head, but at the time I didn't know how to discern between correct messages and false ones.

The psychic information we bring through for people comes in from many different sources, and it is important to discern where it's coming from. Don't be naïve about the spirits who will communicate with you, since some will indeed give you bad or hurtful information. Most people in the beginning of their development attract earthbound spirits because both parties are so anxious to communicate. Whenever you open up to do psychic work, you need to ask your guides for help and make it clear (by stating it out loud) that you want no earthbound spirits channeling any information.

Eventually you'll be able to tell by the quality of the information if it's coming from a guide or a ghost. As you grow psychically, this gets easier because you'll know the feel of your guides versus other spirits around you. You'll be able to feel if the source of the information is a positive, clear, detached soul, or if the source has a hidden agenda, such as a deceased loved one trying to control someone's life.

SOURCES OF THE INFORMATION

When we receive psychic information, it can come from several sources. Our spirit guides and guardian angels bring us information, and these spirits get information on another person by communicating either with the person's guides or with his or her soul. Sometimes our deceased loved ones bring through information, as do the deceased loved ones of the people we're reading. Earthbound spirits (ghosts) make feeble attempts at sending messages to us, and of course God gives us messages for ourselves and others.

ASKING FOR ACCURACY

Before I begin a reading, I ask God to work through me and give me clear, accurate information that will help the client understand him- or herself better. I ask for help with interpreting the visions accurately and help that I hear my guides clearly. I always thank God and my guides before the information begins to flow, and then I focus on the white light within my solar plexus and wait for the information to come.

It's important to remember that we're not doing this alone. We are relying on outside help, so I think it's important to acknowledge and thank our guides. And always, always, pray for accuracy.

BOUNDARIES

Do you know what the phrase "personal boundaries" means? Personal boundaries are all the areas of our lives that should be respected as private. Our homes, property, and material possessions are private. Our personal business such as mail and emails are private. The things in our purses and wallets are private. The thoughts and feelings we write in our journals are private.

As psychics, it's very important that we respect people's privacy. When I do a reading for someone, I always ask what areas of the person's life he or she wants me to look at. I get very specific because I'm not going to look at something the person doesn't want me to. If a woman asks me to look at her marriage, I ask her what areas of her marriage she wants me to focus on. If a man asks about his health, I ask if there's a specific area of his body he's concerned about. Some people tell me to just go ahead and tell them whatever I see, but I won't do this. The client has to direct me or I won't go there, and the reason is simple.

When I first started giving psychic readings, I read things about people that I assumed they wanted to know about, but that wasn't always the case. People would get upset and tell me that they hadn't wanted me to go there. Health problems, marital infidelity, financial concerns: You may consider the information important or harmless, but you have no way of knowing for sure, so it's best to have the client or friend direct the reading. We need to respect each person's personal boundaries.

Another thing that pops up a lot in psychic readings is that people will ask you to read private information about someone else in their life. In almost every reading I do, the client asks about some other person in his or her life, whether it's a significant other, a parent, a child, a boss or coworker, an employee, a neighbor, or a recent acquaintance. We humans seem inherently curious about each other, and sometimes as psychics we can get information for people regarding their relationships and sometimes we can't. In this case, you're the one who has to set the boundaries and let the person know if giving this information doesn't feel right. You are putting yourself in the position of violating someone's personal boundaries without consent. It is very important to have integrity in your work.

For all these reasons, and I can't emphasize this strongly enough, it's essential to have integrity in your work. But the other reason why it's so important to respect people's boundaries and privacy is karma. Karma is the "golden rule" in action: it basically means that whatever you do to someone else will be done to you. If you violate someone's privacy, your privacy will be violated in one way or another. It's that simple! From a karmic standpoint, you want to remember that all of your actions are recorded in your soul. If you abuse others with your psychic abilities, such as scamming them, trying to control or manipulate them, or lying to them so that somehow you'll benefit, *you* will eventually pay the consequences because of it. The law of karma applies to everyone.

PEOPLE CAN PSYCHICALLY BLOCK YOU

Every once in a while, when I am trying to read someone, I get a picture of a big X, a brick wall, a circle with a slash through it, or a blanket. These are my symbols for "no." While the symbols for no that you get may be different, they mean one of the following things, and you need to respect it:

1) The person has consciously or subconsciously put a privacy fence around him- or herself, and the person doesn't want to be read.

2) The information that the person is asking about might not be any of his or her business.

3) Or it could mean that the person is not supposed to have any information regarding his or her particular concern at this time.

Whenever I get one of my symbols for no, I ask my guides what's up. If it's the last reason, I ask when the timing would be better for the person to get a reading.

As hard as this is to understand, sometimes we have to go through tough situations in life without an explanation as to why. Often the reason is that we're supposed to go through the experience on blind faith, eventually learning that we'll be okay no matter what happens.

Sometimes people think that if you get one of these pictures symbolizing no, that means bad news or that they're going to die, but I've never known this to be the case.

I've had clients offer to pay me more money if I could find a way to get past the blocks and read the intimate details of another person's thoughts and feelings, but I'm not in the detective business, and this isn't about invading other people's privacy. If a picture comes up that indicates a block when you ask about something or someone, respect it and move on to the next question.

GROUNDING

One of the definite disadvantages of being psychic is that we can get pretty spacey and feel completely ungrounded. This happens because we're opening up to different dimensions of reality, and the higher up we go, the spacier we can feel. As we continue to grow psychically, we have longer communications with guides and deeper meditations, which can make us feel very light. Psychics have a tendency to be overweight, and I think one of the reasons is that they feel uncomfortable with the lightness they experience when doing their work or meditating, and they create a heaviness in their bodies to make them feel more grounded, more anchored to the earth. I've noticed many times that after doing a reading I grab for sugar, and this is because the taste in my mouth and the sugar rush in my body both help me feel grounded.

To "ground yourself," you can do basically anything that reminds you that you are living in a human body on this planet. Getting in contact with the earth itself is very effective. Whatever you do, make sure it engages as many of your senses as possible: touch, taste, smell, hearing, sight. The more senses you have going, the more grounded you'll feel.

Being psychic does not mean that you are doomed to being overweight or going through life as a space cadet. Here are some specific things you can do to feel grounded:

1) Exercise is a great way to feel grounded. Not only does it awaken your body, but you have to stay mentally in your body if for no other reason than to avoid dropping weights on your foot or flying off the treadmill.

2) Eat a meal with heavy foods, such as meat, potatoes, chocolate, oatmeal, and so on. Choose whatever gives your stomach that full feeling.

3) For me, after doing an intense reading or several in one day, sometimes the best thing I can do for myself is to go to a shopping mall or supermarket and walk around. I take in all the colors and smells and stay very conscious of where I am. However, some psychics find malls the opposite of grounding, so you'll have to try both and see which way works best for you.

4) Showers or baths can help you get focused. *Feel the water* on your body.

5) Movies that get you into your feelings, such as laughter, sadness, joy, or anger, help you feel grounded.

6) Go outdoors and experience nature. Touch the trees, the grass, the dirt. Feel the sun. Breath the fresh air and smell the flowers.

7) Carry rocks around in your pockets.

8) Sex will keep you in your body and focused on being here (as long as it is not abusive sex).

9) Engage in a favorite hobby or any manual activity that requires your concentration.

10) Working at a computer is *not* very grounding. If you're feeling spacey, be sure to get up and do something physical from time to time.

11) Playing music, singing, and dancing are all grounding.

12) Try this visualization: imagine roots coming out of the bottom of your feet and going deep into the earth. This will help you feel more anchored.

PROTECTING YOURSELF PSYCHICALLY

Another downfall of being psychic is that you're more sensitive to people and the world around you. Oftentimes you will feel people's emotional, mental, and physical pain simply by thinking of them or being around them, and because of this level of sensitivity, you will have to make a concentrated effort to protect yourself so that you can function in the world as normally as possible.

The one psychic ability that can be particularly bothersome is clairsentience, or the gift of sensing. There's a fine line between using clairsentience to read people or situations and becoming a "psychic sponge."

Psychic Sponge

Psychic sponges literally soak up the emotional or physical feelings of the people around them and sometimes even of the world in general.

If you are not sure whether you are one of these people who seems to pick up everyone else's "stuff," answer the following questions. After spending five minutes with a crabby friend, do you feel crabby? After having a quick conversation with your boss, who happens to have a headache, do you end up with a headache? If you visit a neighbor who's suffering from depression, do you walk away feeling depressed? Have you ever run into a friend at the grocery store who was very angry over something, and then you wound up feeling angry for the rest of the day? If any of these describes you, the good news is that you have clairsentience. The bad news is that you are unwittingly soaking up everyone else's feelings and acting like a psychic sponge.

Help is on the way!

Have no fear. Help is on the way. I have a couple of simple tips that will help protect you from soaking up everyone else's vibes. And the number one suggestion is . . . buy some sponges!

I have a dear friend who is every bit a psychic sponge (as are many of my students), and she was affected by it in every area of her life. She was always soaking up so much random energy that she had a hard time discerning whether it was her own emotions she was feeling or someone else's. I gave her the clearing exercise (see below), but it wasn't enough. One day in meditation I asked my inner voice what would be helpful for her. The message came to send her sponges that she could put around her house. One by her phone so that whenever she was talking to someone, the sponge would soak up the energy coming from the other end of the line. One by her computer to soak up the energy coming from her screen. One by her front door to soak up the energy of people who came to visit. One in her car to absorb the energy she would pick up from other drivers. One by her bed so that she could get a good night's sleep. My guides even suggested putting a small piece of a sponge inside her bra or pocket. Finally, I was told that once a week, if not more often, she should clear the sponges by rinsing them in water that contained sea salt.

I mailed her some sponges along with these instructions, and she noticed that having the sponges around visibly reminded her to do the clearing exercise as well. She began doing this on a regular basis, and it made a big difference in her life. She is no longer soaking up everyone else's energy and doesn't feel like she's bouncing off the walls with all of this scattered energy in her body. It's made it a lot easier for her to distinguish her own feelings.

If you sound as sensitive as my friend, I strongly suggest that you buy some sponges and put them around your home and office. As goofy as this sounds, it really is a simple, effective little tool. Then, once or twice a week, put one teaspoon sea salt in two cups of water and soak the sponges in this water. As the sponges are soaking, simply ask the Universe to clear all the negative energy from them. Then rinse them out and put them back where you had them.

PROTECTION EXERCISES

Here are some more suggestions for how you can protect yourself psychically. Are you one of those people who has a tough time being in public because the vibes are so intense? My psychic brother Michael doesn't go to any sporting events because the vibes of all the people at the stadiums are sometimes too much for him to be around. He rarely shops at malls and doesn't go to concerts because he feels like he absorbs the energy. When he has gone to public events, he ends up feeling scattered and ungrounded for two to three days afterwards.

Whether you are ultra-sensitive or semi-sensitive, I have a few simple suggestions as to how you can psychically protect yourself.

Clearing Exercise

My guides have told me that all people go through their days picking up energy from other people, and that at the end of each day, our auras (the energy field around our body) look like decorated Christmas trees. They said our auras need to be cleared in order for us to feel clear, like running the lint remover over our clothes. This clearing exercise is very effective and should be used by everyone, whether you are clairsentient or not.

Get into the habit of doing this exercise throughout your day and before crawling into bed. If necessary, write it down on a piece of paper and carry it with you. Get in the habit of saying it whenever you're feeling kind of "off."

To begin, close your eyes and take a couple of nice relaxing breaths. Then simply ask God or the Universe to clear you:

Please clear my mind
Clear my mind
Please clear my body
Clear my body
Please clear my soul
Clear my soul
Please clear me psychically
Clear me psychically

You can also be more specific, adding any or all of the following anytime you want:

Please clear my home
Clear my home
Please clear my work area
Clear my work area
Please clear my bed
Clear my bed
(Or, clear my car, clear my pet, and so on)

You should notice a change in things right away. I tell my students the first night of class that even if they never come back and decide never to develop their abilities, I want them to always do the clearing exercise because it's so helpful for anyone living on this planet. You don't have to be a psychic sponge to pick up other people's energy, and it can be a real burden if you don't know what to do about it.

PSYCHIC PROTECTION

Clear Bubble

This exercise is for people who are claustrophobic, because you can see through the bubble. Using your imagination, visualize yourself surrounded by a bubble of strong see-through polyurethane, like an adult-size plastic baggie with the zipper zipped up! Get in the habit of visualizing this whenever you go out of the house, and you'll be surprised at how much more you can do without being psychically or physically affected.

Eggshell

Whenever you're feeling especially vulnerable, I would suggest visualizing yourself surrounded by a shell, such as an eggshell with no cracks or holes in it. This seems to be even more protective than the invisible bubble because on a psychic level you're putting up a very visible shield that separates you from others.

Purple Cape

This visualization has come to me in many of the meditations I've done for my students regarding psychic protection. Using your imagination, visualize a floor-length purple cape with a hood on it; the inside of the cape is turquoise. Visualize putting this on and zipping up the front. Purple is a very strong, protective color that is heavier and therefore more grounding, and turquoise is very similar but with a lighter vibration. The combination of these two colors is very good protection, so whenever you're feeling vulnerable, visualize wearing this cape on your body.

Just because we, as psychics, are extra sensitive to the things that go on in our world doesn't mean we have to grin and bear it. If you find it almost impossible to be around groups of people because of all the intense vibes, don't let your sensitivity continue to be a hindrance. Get in the habit of doing the clearing exercise and putting up one of these forms of protection. There's no need to feel victimized by your sensitivity and gifts. We do have choices.

PSYCHIC ATTACK

I hate to even mention "psychic attacks" because some people can get so freaked out about whether or not they are being psychically attacked by someone. However, if you feel that someone is sending you negative energy, such as negative thoughts or wishes, here is a very simple suggestion that *works:* either mentally visualize putting up mirrors facing away from you or actually do this. Then the person's thoughts will either go back to the person or out into the Universe. You can also ask the Universe to dispel any negative energy that comes at you.

Here's an example of how I've found the mirrors to be helpful: I was trying to do a reading for a man whose wife didn't want him to get one. Though I don't think she was doing it intentionally, her angry vibes were coming at me very strongly, and they were blocking me from reading him. I literally took a mirror out of my purse and put it on the chair facing away from me. It immediately stopped the flow of negative energy coming at me, and I was able to do his reading.

If there's someone in your life who is hateful, angry, jealous, or spiteful toward you, whenever that person's name comes into your head, ask the Universe to clear you of any negative thoughts he or she might be consciously or unconsciously sending you. If you feel like you're being psychically attacked or "slimed" by someone, simply put up mirrors and ask the Universe to clear both of you of the negative vibes and to bless both of you. If you would prefer to have twenty-four-hour protection, choose one of the protection suggestions above and you should be just fine.

TWO NO-NOS

No Drugs or Alcohol

I would suggest not doing psychic exercises when you've been doing drugs or drinking. Psychically gifted people are very sensitive as it is, and adding mind-altering chemicals can leave you very vulnerable. While it's true that some mind-altering experiences can be quite interesting, to say the least, you run the risk of attracting "undesirables" to you, such as earthbound spirits who were addicted to drugs or alcohol when they were living. This is the last thing you need. For more information, I suggest picking up a copy of my books *Relax, It's Only a Ghost* and *Dear Echo* and reading about possession.

If you have a serious problem with alcohol or drugs, you really shouldn't be opening yourself up psychically at all, since you could be inviting a variety of psychic experiences that you might not be able to deal with. Wait until you've gotten into sobriety and laid a spiritual foundation for yourself. Then you'll be more equipped to handle whatever comes along.

Avoid Bad Weather

For the first couple years of your development, I strongly suggest that you don't open up psychically if you're experiencing bad weather or it's predicted for that day. Talk about feeling ungrounded. Low or high barometric pressure can make us feel "off center" or spacier than normal. We can easily pick up the energy in the atmosphere, and depending upon what's going on, it can make us feel very distracted. If there's a lot of intense energy, like tornado weather, we *can* feel it in our bodies and it *can* feel like a caged lion. When you have intense weather, I strongly recommend that you try one of the three psychic protection exercises above, and hopefully you won't be affected by it.

Chapter 5

Understanding Psychic Information

Responsibility can be frightening. I currently have a student who definitely has psychic abilities, but she's very afraid of them. When she took my beginner class, she'd come for the lecture portion and leave before we did the exercises. She'd always tell me she didn't have any psychic abilities and that she didn't want them either. I asked her if she was able to pinpoint her resistance, and she said it was the responsibility that terrified her. She didn't want to see negative information about people or disasters.

Two or three times she did stay and tried the exercises. She was always accurate with the information that came through her, but then she'd get so freaked out that she'd stop coming to class for a couple of weeks. Two days before the 9/11 terrorist attacks, she kept getting a picture of a plane crashing, but she didn't know what it meant. She became extremely anxious because she wasn't sure if it was a warning about one of her loved ones or if it was a prophetic vision of something to come.

Shutting the door on your psychic abilities because you're afraid of the responsibilities associated with these gifts is understandable, but I encourage you to keep the door open and learn how to discern and work with the information.

I've seen this happen with other students who have prophetic visions that frighten them. The students think that if they stop coming to class, their third eye will shut down and the visions will stop, but that's not how it goes. I always encourage students to hang in there and understand their visions rather than try to deny them. As they soon learn, denying them doesn't stop them.

Not all psychics get prophetic visions of disasters, and I've found that the ones who do get them have been getting them on and off for most of their life. It isn't psychic development that makes a person have prophetic visions. It's psychic development that helps you understand them, and that helps you distinguish between visions that are truly prophetic and those that are actually the products of your fears or ego.

PROPHETIC VISIONS, FEAR, AND EGO

I want you to think about what fear feels like. It's usually located in the stomach area, and it has a strong energy to it — it's that sinking feeling in the pit of your stomach that spreads quickly throughout your whole body. Sometimes people mistake this feeling with intuition because they're both located in the same area, but this feeling does *not* indicate your intuition. Intuition does not have any emotion attached to it. It simply gives us information.

Often when people are just developing their psychic abilities, they haven't learned how to discern between a true vision, a fear, or a picture that their ego might be creating, and this can be very frightening. Students often tell me about previous experiences when they thought they were receiving an intuitive message or a psychic prediction, only to find out it was one of their fears, or it was their ego wanting to impress someone with "psychic information."

Here is a very simple but effective technique to help you understand which of the three your vision might be: First, do the clearing exercise to help you clear the information from your head and the fear from your body. Ask yourself how the information came to you. Did it simply pop into your head out of nowhere? If so, then it might have been a true vision, but also ask yourself: Is it related to anything you might have seen on TV or in the newspaper the day before? Did it feel fearful when you saw it in your mind? It's very important that you calm yourself down and determine the source of the information. Some of my students saw visions of airplanes going into buildings after the 9/11 terrorist attacks, and they thought that these were predictions of more attacks coming.

But when I had them trace back the feelings associated with these visions, they discovered their fears were creating these pictures.

In a similar way, say you're planning to take a car trip, and the day before you leave, you get images of a car crash and everyone dying. The vision feels really scary, and afterward your body is racing with adrenaline. What have you just seen?

First things first, calm yourself down. Ask yourself, are these images similar to anything you've seen in the media lately? Has someone you know recently been in a wreck? The fact that the information came with an adrenaline rush of fear should tell you that this "vision" is connected to fears concerning the trip. If it was a psychic prediction, you would have been given the information without any emotion attached. You would have seen an accident (clairvoyance), thoughts would have come into your mind of the car breaking down (clairaudience), or you would have had an inner knowingness that something was wrong, a simple certainty that you weren't supposed to go on the trip (intuition). These would have all arrived as plain information. Another interesting distinction between real and manufactured visions is this: when our mind creates a vision, the images go on and on and seem to get more elaborate with time, whereas a psychic message comes quickly and is gone. My teacher always told us to pay attention when spirits speak because they don't repeat themselves!

In other words, here is what to look for:

1) If it's a prophetic vision (even a negative one), it will simply be a picture that came in out of nowhere, with no emotion attached to it.

2) If it's one of your fears, you'll be very aware of fear as you're seeing the pictures. They will seem to go hand in hand. Fear also multiplies quickly and can easily create a hundred scary scenarios in a matter of seconds, so beware.

3) If it's a picture your ego has created (in its desire to experience a "psychic vision"), your mind will be racing with thoughts, and there will be mixed feelings of excitement and fear. Our ego likes to be the hero, so from time to time it might try to come up with "psychic information" in order to bedazzle people.

Ask for the Truth

One of the coolest things about our intuition is that it will show us the truth of any situation whenever we ask (so long as our agenda isn't in the way). If you've gotten some information and aren't sure what to do with it, try this visualization: Find a quiet place away from the noises of the world and sit down. Close your eyes and take three or four relaxing breaths. Focus on the area of your solar plexus. Inside is a white light at the center of your soul. I think of it as the light of God within. Using your imagination, visualize this light and completely focus your attention on it. Take a few more relaxing breaths, and with each breath, imagine this light getting bigger and brighter until it completely surrounds you. Feel the peacefulness of the light. This is a very good discipline to learn in any case because it is a simple technique that you will use over and over in your psychic work.

Once your mind has calmed down, and you're able to focus only on this light, tell your inner voice to show you the truth of the situation. Ask it if the information that came to you is accurate. If it is, you'll get an inner knowing of yes. Then, while continuing to focus on the light, ask if there's anything you should do about it. If your mind starts to race with thoughts and ideas, return your focus to the calmness of the white light.

If the answer is no, you will either get a no feeling or it will feel blank. If that's the case, thank the light for guiding you and open your eyes *when you feel done.*

Some students protest that they aren't good at visualizing and they can't see this light, but hear me loud and clear: You have an imagination and you *can* imagine this light. You're not even making it up because we all have this light within our soul. You may have to use your imagination in the beginning to open your mind to this idea, but after you've done this a few times, it will become very natural to see the light inside.

Use Your Journal

You may find that no answers come when you're doing this visualization, but over the course of the next few days, more information may come when you least expect it. I would strongly suggest any time you get information and you're not sure what to do with it, record it in your psychic journal. You may indeed have picked up on an impending situation through your psychic abilities. But even if not, writing in your psychic journal can be very helpful. Recording the visions, thoughts, and intuitive feelings can help you sort through what's fact or fiction, ego or fear. You can review the things you've previously written and get a better understanding of the meaning of the pictures, images, and feelings you've received. This is how we learn to discern truth from nontruth, the feeling of accurate psychic information from the feeling of random thoughts, fearful imaginings, and self-created visions. This is how we establish accuracy.

LEARNING TO RECEIVE

In the beginning of your development, focus simply on learning how to receive the thoughts and pictures coming into your "psychic center," and worry about understanding them later. Before you begin doing psychic readings, you need to open up your third eye and psychic ears, and you need to learn how to get yourself out of the way. This seems simple, but every beginner struggles with it, and the main reason is because we all fear being wrong. You get past that fear by practicing with someone you trust. You're going to be taking a lot of risks with this person and you don't want to have to worry about being criticized. In chapter 6, I provide you with four exercises for practicing; all of them require working with a trusted partner. When I was just beginning to develop my own abilities, the first time I ever did one of these exercises in a class (the psychometry exercise), my partner gave me a fountain pen. I held it in my hand, and into my head came a picture of a bag of apples. My first thought was to blow it off because it seemed so insignificant, and I didn't want to say anything stupid. Unfortunately, every time I concentrated on my third eye, I saw this bag of apples. Then I saw a porch with a rocking chair. My rational mind argued that these images had nothing to do with a pen, and so I discounted them.

When my teacher came over, she asked me what information I was getting. Because I didn't want to be laughed at, I told her I wasn't getting anything. She asked me what the bag of apples were if I wasn't seeing anything, and it totally freaked me out. She said that I had to tell my partner everything I was seeing and feeling because this was the only way I was going to learn how to discern between psychic information and my own random thoughts. She also said I had to get my ego out of the way and stop worrying about being wrong. For me, this was a whole lot easier said than done. I told my partner the images that were coming to me: the bag of apples, a porch with a rocking chair, and an apple orchard. He said that the pen had belonged to his grandfather, who owned an apple orchard, and that he used to sit in his rocking chair on the front porch of his farm and look out over his apple trees. I was blown away. I was also grateful that my teacher pushed me to say the things I was seeing, hearing, and feeling.

Since I can't be there to push you, you are going to have to push yourself. Tell your partner everything, all of the images, thoughts, and feelings that come to you. Be willing to be completely wrong (and this is why it's important to work with someone you trust). This is the only way you will be able to learn what accurate information feels like. There are also practical reasons for you to say everything you're seeing as it happens. One is that sometimes no new information will come until you've given the person what you've already received. Another is that sometimes the information comes very fast, and you must quickly relay what you're seeing in order to keep up with it. If you're too busy thinking about what's happening, and let your ego and fears of being wrong get in the way, you might miss important information.

Wear It like a Loose Garment

The other bit of advice I have for those who are just beginning is to *wear the information like a loose garment.* Until you learn more about interpretation and the various forms of psychic information, don't take anything you receive too seriously at first. If you're in your first year of development and you do start doing minireadings for people, be sure to tell them you're still in training. Once in a while, a newly graduated student will get some business cards made up at the end of my thirteen-week class because the person thinks he or she is ready to start doing readings for a living. There is so much to learn about interpreting and understanding these gifts that there is no way a person could be ready that quickly. I practiced on friends and family members for twelve years before doing this work full-time. That doesn't mean it's going to take you that long, but it will take time. If you're in a crummy job and are hoping to develop your abilities so you can set up shop as a psychic instead, I suggest you find a different job while you're taking the time to develop your gifts. You don't need the added pressure of having to develop your gifts quickly, and it will just interfere with your development anyway.

INTUITION, YOUR GREATEST HELPER

Using your intuition is a very important part of your psychic development and of your psychic work. Your intuition will always let you know if you're on the right track with your interpretation of psychic information. I always rely on my inner voice when doing a reading. If I get a picture I can't interpret, I go right to my intuition and start asking it questions: Is this how I should interpret the picture? What does this mean? I ask my intuition for clarity all the time.

Here's one of my goofy little pictures for you. Imagine the pit in a peach. Now imagine having one of those deep inside your soul. Within that seed is a silent voice of truth and clarity, which is a way of saying that this voice speaks to us more through an inner knowing than with an actual voice. You know that feeling you get in your gut when you just *know* something? You just *knew* so and so was going to call, or you just *knew* that you should've turned left instead of right? This silent voice of *knowing* is our intuition, and it comes from the divine within each of us. This inner knowing will never lie to you, and its guidance is 100 percent accurate.

If you're already accustomed to living by this inner voice, you know just how helpful it can be. If this whole concept is new to you, I suggest getting a copy of my book *A Still Small Voice: A Psychic's Guide to Awakening Intuition.* This will be your best helper when it comes to interpreting psychic information accurately. I can't say enough about the accuracy and integrity that intuition will bring to your work. It will not only help you as a psychic but in every area of your life.

DEVELOPING CLAIRAUDIENCE

Clairaudience is the gift of hearing, and this means that spirit communicates to us through thought. It would be fairly easy to understand and interpret these thoughts if they sounded like distinct voices, but they don't. Their thoughts sound similar to our own, and so the discernment takes time to develop. Learning how to do this requires you to take some risks because when a thought pops into your head, you'll have to run it by the person you're practicing with to see if it's a clairaudient message or one of your thoughts. I guarantee that if you really work at learning how to discern between the two, you will be able to tell the difference between thoughts coming into you clairaudiently and your own thoughts.

Even after doing this for thirty-seven years, I sometimes run the information by the client to see if I'm on the right track because the information can be difficult to discern. I've gotten used to the guides that work with me and recognize their thoughts, but when there's a different energy I may not be able to make a quick judgment. The other energy might be the client's own spirit guides, their deceased relatives, or their souls sending me the information. If this is the case, I'm not used to these vibrations and sometimes I need to check it out with the client. At first, anyway, you should share everything with your partner.

DEVELOPING CLAIRVOYANCE

Psychic information can arrive in the form of pictures or visions, and clairvoyance is the gift of seeing these images. These pictures come into your third eye, which is located in the middle of your forehead.

When I was growing up, I thought crystal balls and tea leaves had psychic information inside, and that when a gypsy gazed into these things, they were creating these amazing pictures that foretold someone's future. Even though this didn't make logical sense to me, I couldn't figure out where else the information could be coming from. It never occurred to me that these objects were simply a focal point allowing physical eyes to focus on something while psychic pictures come into the gypsy's third eye.

When I finally grasped how clairvoyance worked, I realized that the crystal ball or the tea leaves could just as well be a hockey puck. As you practice receiving clairvoyant images, choose some simple object for your physical eyes to focus on so that you won't get distracted by your surroundings. Staring at a wall, the floor, or keeping your eyes closed all work equally well.

Steps to developing clairvoyance:

1) Opening the third eye

2) Receiving the pictures

3) Accurately interpreting the information you're receiving.

INTERPRETING WHAT YOU SEE

Perhaps the most important part of giving psychic information is how we're interpreting what we're seeing. I believe we get the information accurately, but it's how we interpret the information that can make or break a psychic message for someone.

Interpretation for Clairvoyants

Interpreting clairvoyant images gets easier the longer you work at it, so have patience. One way to think of it is that it is like reading a cartoon strip without any words. The pictures are sometimes literal (a man running up a hill means that the client is going to have to run up a hill) and other times symbolic (the client has to overcome a difficult obstacle). The clairvoyant's job is to interpret both.

Unlike dream books that interpret the pictures for us, there isn't any such book for clairvoyants because the pictures mean different things to different people. Here are some examples to help you understand this easier:

A friend asks you whether or not he will get the job he just applied for. You open your third eye and see one or more of the following:

A door opening
A paycheck
Your friend wearing a new suit
A door closing
Your friend reading the want ads
A Mayflower truck

A client asks you to look at her health, specifically her lungs. Here are some pictures you might see:

Black coals in a chimney

A clear day

Mold

Climbing up a very steep mountain

A hospital

A coffin

A clean bill of health

The word "bronchitis"

The word "asthma"

A friend asks how soon it's going to be before he meets Ms. Right. Here are some pictures that relate to timing:

A lot of snow on the ground

Colored leaves on the trees

Little buds on trees

A calendar with the first initial of the month, such as J, D, or A

Fireworks going off

Numbers, such as 2, 3, or 4

An astrology sign

The same friend asks you to describe Ms. Right, and here are some of the pictures you might get:

The face of someone you know

An old picture frame

Someone tall or short

Dark hair

A runner or athlete

A bottle of beer

Someone checking her watch

A doctor's coat

A teddy bear

Stacks of books

Fishing

A broken heart

Keeping Interpretation Simple

When interpreting pictures, it is important to remember to look at the various meanings and their simplest forms. The guides are going to give you kindergarten-level pictures to make it as easy as possible for you to grasp the meaning of their messages. You might think, given the simple nature of these pictures, that you couldn't possibly misinterpret them. On the contrary, your intellect will often go in the opposite direction, looking for the most complicated interpretations. That's why you should run all your interpretations by your intuition, which will let you know if you're on the right track. Don't be in a hurry. Accuracy is everything.

Here are the interpretations that I've gotten regarding some of these pictures. For example, the health pictures: When I saw the vision of black coals in a chimney, I asked my intuition several questions about it, and I got that it meant the client had cancer (which was later confirmed). When I got a clear day, it was pretty obvious; the person was fine. When I've gotten a coffin, it usually symbolizes death or the ending of something. The image of climbing up a steep hill meant that the person had a long road ahead to restore her health.

USING PERSONAL SYMBOLS TO MAKE IT EASIER

When our guides answer a question about someone's personality, they sometimes give us a picture of someone we know. This is their way of saying that the person in question has similar characteristics to the person we know. Using the example above, if your friend asked you to describe what his Ms. Right would be like and you got an image of your neighbor Judy, it would mean that the woman would be similar in personality to Judy. Instead of giving you all kinds of different pictures to describe your friend's Ms. Right, your guides will be more efficient and use a shorthand they know you'll understand: Judy. Your job is to determine which characteristics are similar. These characteristics will usually be the first things you think of when you think of "Judy": perhaps chatty, friendly, hard worker, gardener, writer.

You'll need to ask your intuition for assistance in discerning which characteristics are accurate. Is Ms. Right chatty? Yes. Is she friendly? Strong yes. Is she hard working? Yes. Family oriented? A "no" response. A gardener? Yes. And so on.

Timing

People ask timing questions all the time: How soon will I meet my soul mate? When will I get married? When will I get a job? When should I go on vacation? When will my alcoholic spouse quit drinking? When will I get pregnant? When will my health improve? When will my sickly parent die? Questions like these come up all the time, and our job is to pin our guides down to exact times.

Timing questions are always interesting, and tricky, because we're asking spirits who don't go by timing to put everything into our earthly time frame. They do the best they can, but getting them to be very specific isn't easy. When they give you a number, such as 2, 3, or 4, your job is to discern if that means hours, days, weeks, months, or years. Sometimes they'll give you a number, and when you ask for more information, they might give you a picture that represents a season, such as snow on the ground or colored leaves in the fall. If you get one of these season pictures, pay close attention to the details. Is there a lot of snow on the ground or just a little bit? Are the colored leaves on the trees or on the ground? Are the baby buds on the trees just coming out or are they ready to blossom? These details will help you fine-tune when the event will occur.

If you're clairaudient, you might hear the word "soon," but don't take this at face value. Keep hunting for more specific information because "soon" to a spirit who lives without clocks and calendars could be tomorrow or ten years from now! I can't tell you the number of clients who have come back to me a year or two after their reading to tell me that everything that was predicted came true, but the timing was off.

A friend of mine who is in the process of opening up her third eye recently said that communicating with her guides is like playing charades. They give her a picture, and then she proceeds to play twenty questions with them in order to figure out what the picture means. I couldn't have said it better myself!

Putting the Pieces Together

The more you practice asking questions, the more pictures you'll receive, and then it's like putting together the pieces to a jigsaw puzzle. Once you've done that, you'll need to discern if the pictures are real or symbolic, and again, you do this by enlisting the help of your intuition. It's pretty cool how it all comes together to create messages for people. Here are some examples of how entire messages get put together.

A client wanted to know what the missing piece in her life was, and the image that came was of a woman walking up a rocky hillside trail in Peru in search of mystic monks. My job as the clairvoyant is to figure out if she's really supposed to go to Peru in search of these monks or if this is symbolic of her needing to go on a spiritual quest. I asked my guides, but they simply smiled at me and sent the thought that she'd know soon. I asked my intuition, but it didn't give me any specifics other than that the information was important for her to hear.

Another client asked me why she felt so alone, and the image that came was of a woman living in a tree house. I saw people walking by but no one stopping to say hello. I also noticed that she never looked out the windows. She just sat in the middle of the tree house wondering why she was so alone. To interpret this, I asked the picture some questions. What did the tree house symbolize? Being away from society? *Yes.* Was this something she was creating? Yes. Why was she choosing this way of life? "Fear" was the answer that came into my head. Fear of people, fear of intimacy, fear of what? I asked. The statement that came into my head was "Yes, fear of everything. She isolates herself to protect herself."

When I gave the client the information that she was the one creating the loneliness out of fear, she broke down crying and said she didn't know what to do about it. The next image that came into my head was an office with someone sitting at a desk. I asked my intuition if this was a clergy person and got no response. I asked if this was a counselor and got a strong intuitive feeling of yes. I asked if she knew this person yet, and I got a "no" feeling but heard the words "sister does." I asked the woman if her sister was seeing a therapist, and she said that her sister's neighbor was a therapist. I asked my guides if this was who she should see about healing these fears, and they said yes.

Another client asked me where she should move to, and I saw an image of a friend of mine who lives in Scottsdale, Arizona. I asked the client if Scottsdale was one of the places she was thinking of moving to, and she said that Scottsdale was her first choice. (Some images are easier to figure out than others!)

A client asked how soon it would be before he found a job. First, I got an image of a piggy bank full of money. The next image was of him holding it upside down and shaking out the last penny. Then I saw a picture of him sitting at a desk shuffling papers. After questioning my intuition, I interpreted this image sequence to mean that he would not get a job until he had used up all of his savings.

Finally, here is a more complicated example, in which I needed to ask the pictures and my guides a lot of questions in order to get the full message: A client told me she was having difficulty getting pregnant, and the doctors thought it was because her husband had lazy sperm and they weren't making the journey to her eggs. She wanted me to take a look and see if this was the problem. The first image came of a womb holding up a sign that said, "Keep out." This indicated to me that it wasn't the husband's sperm but the woman's body that was having the problem. I had a dialogue with this picture. I asked her body what the problem was and into my head came the words "She never takes care of me, so I don't want to have to take care of a baby." I asked the womb what the woman could do in order to get pregnant, and I heard the statement "If she took time out for me [her body] and took better care of me, *then* I would be willing to get pregnant." Then I had a vision of a woman carrying a baby and sitting at an executive desk, with her hair all haggard and her face looking tired. The next image was a big NO over this picture. So I asked the womb if this meant that the body wasn't up to "having it all," and I heard the word "prioritize." I asked the womb if this meant that the woman had to prioritize what was important and eliminate the things in her life that were draining her energy, and I saw an image of a bingo parlor and someone calling out, "Bingo!" That's a picture I often get when my guides are telling me I've accurately interpreted the pictures.

Even after all this, I wanted to make doubly sure I was accurately reading the whole message, so I spelled it out to my guides. I asked: If the woman took better care of herself, figured out what her priorities were and stuck to them, and then made room in her life for a baby, would she get pregnant then? The image that came into my mind was of the womb, but now the "Keep out" sign was gone; to me, this indicated yes. Finally, I also checked this interpretation out with my intuition, and my intuition gave me a positive nudge.

EXAMPLES OF MISINTERPRETATION

Whenever we misinterpret information, it's usually because we assume the meaning of an image too quickly. Sometimes we make assumptions based on the way the client asked the question, and sometimes we pick up the desires of the client. Sometimes the images seem so obvious we don't bother to question our guides or intuition any further. Here are some examples of how easy it is to misinterpret what we see.

A client asked me in the springtime when I saw her father's health improving. The image that came was of an outdoor garden. I saw a big lawn, freshly mowed, with lots of people milling around a big table of food. Her dad seemed to be the focus of a lot of the conversations going on. I asked my guides when this was, and they showed me a calendar with a month beginning with J. I asked my intuition if this was June, and I got a no. I asked if it was July, and got yes. I assumed all of this meant he would be better by July, and that the image was of some sort of outdoor garden party to celebrate it. You can probably see what's coming, but I didn't. I told my client this, and she left very relieved. Then she called me in July to tell me she had just returned from her father's funeral. She said they had held the luncheon outside in a friend's yard! I felt awful to say the least. This is a case where I asked the wrong question — I only asked when her father's health would improve, not *if* — and I didn't stop to verify whether my interpretation of the answer was correct.

Here's another example, this one with a happier outcome: A client asked me if her husband was having an affair. I got an image of a man walking into an office, and I saw a blonde sitting at the receptionist desk. The blond was very flirty, and I could feel a strong sexual energy between them. If I would have stopped there, I would have assumed that the answer was yes — he was having an affair with a blonde in an office. Instead, because I knew it could be quite harmful if I got it wrong, I asked the picture to tell me more.

I saw the man go into his office and shut the door. Intuitively, this felt like the part of the message that was most important. I asked if they were having an affair and saw the word "no" in big letters. I asked if this was simple flirting, and I got a big yes. Then I saw another picture of the husband closing his office door.

I told the client exactly what I was seeing and feeling, and she smiled with a sense of relief. She said that her husband and the receptionist in his office had had an affair at one time, but that he now claimed that it was over between them. She was very happy to have that confirmed.

Sometimes I shudder to think of the damage we can do to people and their lives if we misinterpret the information. We have to be so careful all the time.

Predicting the Sex of a Baby

It is easy to mistake the sex of a baby because there are a lot of different things we could be reading. We could pick up on the strong desires of the parents. We could pick up on the strong female hormones coming from the mother's body and interpret that to mean a female child. We could pick up on the soul's sex in its last life! Because I work so much with the soul, this one is hard for me to discern. I'll see the soul who is going to be born, but oftentimes I can't see what sex he or she is going to be in this lifetime. When my brother and his wife were pregnant, I communicated several times with the soul of a young man who was going to incarnate as their baby, and I assumed that this meant the baby was going to be a boy. I was pretty surprised when my niece was born instead.

Months before my son and his wife conceived their baby, a young man's soul came and introduced himself to me. He said he was going to be my grandchild and would be coming soon. When my daughter-in-law found out she was pregnant and didn't want to know the sex of the baby, I decided to experiment. I was on this kick about making baby blankets, and I decided that when I went to the fabric store, I would pick up the blue and pink fleece to see what would happen. Whenever I picked up the blue, I got a really strong feeling to buy it, and whenever I held up the pink, I had a weird aversion to it, like I wanted to put it back right away. Every time I went to the fabric store, I tested the two colors, and my reaction was always the same except for once.

That day, while I was at the fabric store, I got a call on my cell phone from one of my girlfriends, who was calling to tell me that she had just found out that her granddaughter was pregnant. After the call, I went to conduct my fleece experiment and felt this very strong urge to buy pink. At first I panicked, thinking that this must mean that my son and his wife were having twins. Then I thought that maybe all along I had been reading the blue response wrong. Then it occurred to me that maybe I was picking up on the sex of my girlfriend's great-granddaughter, and wouldn't you know, that's exactly what was happening. Her granddaughter gave birth to a little girl, and my son's wife gave birth to a little boy.

My fleece experiment isn't scientific, but you sure could give it a try next time a woman asks you to predict the sex of her baby. You don't even have to go to out. Just imagine yourself standing in a baby store, and then ask your intuition if you should pick up the blue clothes or the pink ones.

Interpreting Symbols of Death

Symbols of death can often be misleading. People assume that whenever they receive a vision of a hearse, a coffin, a skull and crossbones, or a skeleton that it indicates the person in question is about to die. However, it's been my experience that these things usually symbolize the death of a way of life, *not* physical death.

My symbols for death usually come in the form of a diploma, an image of graduation day, of moving day, or of someone simply floating up! In addition, these pictures are almost never heavy and morose, as we might expect of a prediction of death. Instead, they're more carefree, like a bird in flight.

WHAT IF THE MESSAGES ARE WRONG?

At this point, it's important to address another confusing aspect of psychic readings. That is, why is it that information can sometimes be so off?

Sometimes, even when you are certain you are getting a psychic communication, and even when you've been thorough about confirming your interpretation of it, the information you receive will wind up being incorrect. It took me a long time to understand why this could be, since I believed that all psychic communications are true. At first I always assumed I had done something wrong. Instead, what I've come to learn is that sometimes our souls have plans for us that we aren't aware of, and they will sometimes give us false information if it moves us in the right direction.

For a long time, I looked at life only through my humanness and gave very little thought to my soul or "her plan." As I got more and more into my spiritual path and came to believe in reincarnation, I opened up to the idea that you could look at life through the soul's perspective, which is distinct from our conscious mind. When, as I progressed as a psychic, souls began choosing to communicate to me directly, I stumbled into an unexpected difficulty. It was challenging at times to find a way to tell a person's "body" or "conscious mind" information that his or her own soul was communicating to me, and even sometimes withholding from me. Here's an example of what I mean:

A female client wanted to know if a man she had met at a social function — whom she described as the greatest guy she'd ever met — was indeed Mr. Right. Her soul came out of her body during our session and told me to tell her, "Yes, this is the one." Her soul had an odd look on her face, so I knew there must have been something she wasn't sharing. Still, I relayed to the woman what her soul had said. About six months later, the woman came back for another reading. She told me that she had gotten into a relationship with the man, but that it had been the worst relationship she had ever been in. They had since broken up, and she wanted to know why that one part of her last reading was so off.

I asked the woman's soul if she'd be willing to explain, and fortunately she did come out and talk to me. The soul said that she had some hard karma left over from a former lifetime with this particular guy, and she just had to go into the relationship again to pay back the karmic debt. She said that if she had told her conscious mind that it was going to be a difficult relationship that would end badly, she would not have gone into it. I asked my client if this would have been true, and she said yes. The woman also said that when she was in the relationship she had a feeling that what she was going through with him was bigger than both of them and that it wasn't something she could simply walk away from.

Our Soul's Plan

Before we come into a new lifetime, a lot of planning goes on. Our soul will decide on goals it wants to achieve, and there are hundreds of life experiences it may choose to have in order to achieve those goals. For instance, there could be friends, spouses, and family members from past lives that we'll choose to be with either for the support they'll give us or to resolve some unfinished business. It's hard for us to accept the idea that our souls are in charge of our lives rather than ourselves, our minds/bodies, but it's true nevertheless.

If a person goes to a psychic to get a better understanding of why he or she is going through a difficult time, the psychic may only be given what information the person can handle hearing. The soul may choose not to give all the details if it will possibly prevent the person from going through an experience. For instance, a client once asked me if she should invest a large amount of savings in a business with her brother-in-law. In this case, I didn't see her soul. I was given many pictures that indicated yes, yes, yes, this was a really good idea. About a year later, she came back for another reading and said that investing with her brother-in-law had turned out to be a horrible mistake, and she wanted to know why that advice had been so wrong.

I asked her soul if she would be willing to shed any light on the misinformation I'd received, and she said that in a past life in Germany, she and her brother-in-law had been business partners. They were merciless with anyone who was late in making payments, and a lot of people suffered because of their lack of compassion and judgmental attitudes toward anyone with financial difficulties. She said they were both strong, powerful, egotistical men who boasted about their "financial prowess." Her soul said that, in this life, both of them needed to go through what they had just gone through together in order to gain wisdom, compassion, and humility. In spite of their financial knowledge, they made some very foolish decisions that took them down a pretty tough road of financial challenges. They had to deal with creditors who made their life a living hell. The woman said she had gained an immense amount of compassion for anyone who was self-employed, and that she now understood how financial pressure could literally destroy someone. She said that having to file bankruptcy had forced them to let go of a lot of pride they had had about their former financial track record.

If our soul needs to have a certain experience, our guides and our intuition will encourage us to have it. Unfortunately, because society doesn't honor the soul and the bigger picture of our lives, we can end up feeling betrayed by our guides, our intuition, and God when we are led into a painful experience. If only we were taught to look at life through the eyes of our soul, then we would look for the gem in each life experience, however terrible it may seem in the moment, and welcome the benefits we receive from going through them.

Here's Another Twist on Giving the Wrong Information

There's another explanation I've discovered about why people are sometimes given the wrong information, and it is the Universe's way of getting a person "off the fence" in some area of life.

For instance, a young man once asked me if he should marry the young woman he was dating or move on. His guides told me to tell him that he was meant to marry her and that they would have several children. About three weeks after the reading, the young man called to say he was really upset with the information he'd received; after thinking it over, he realized he actually didn't want to marry her, and he wanted me to double-check with his guides to see if they may have "made a mistake."

His guides said that he had been on the fence about the direction of his life, and he needed to be pushed to make some decisions. He needed to really examine what his life would be like if he married this young woman — rather than continuing to tell himself that someday soon he would figure it out — and the information that he was "supposed" to marry her is exactly what he needed in order to do that, and so move on with his life.

I've seen this kind of information come through for people who are stuck in miserable jobs, in bad relationships, or in financial troubles. It's a version of reverse psychology, where guides present advice that is the opposite of what is actually healthy or desired to force the person to "get off the fence," make the right decision, and move forward.

The Other Explanation Is Simply That

Don't forget that the other explanation as to why the information in a psychic reading is off is simply because you misinterpreted the pictures you received or misunderstood the thoughts in your head. You may have interjected your own thoughts rather than actually hearing information from your guides, the person's guides, or his or her soul. More than likely, in the first couple years of your development, this will be the reason that your friend or client says the reading wasn't accurate.

Remember, we are dealing with people's lives, and it's a tremendous responsibility. We are giving them information that could affect the rest of their life. It's important to always remind the person you're reading to check with his or her own intuition as to whether the information you're giving them is correct, and whether he or she should act on what you've said.

Chapter 6

Getting Started with Psychic Development Exercises

Now let's get down to business. In this chapter I will show you how to turn your abilities on and off and then explain four simple exercises that will help you develop and refine your psychic gifts. Besides your desire to explore your psychic abilities, the single most important thing you need at this point is a partner or a group of like-minded people.

Gathering People of a Like Mind

One of the most important ingredients to your development is getting a group of people together who are serious about psychic development. Ask friends and coworkers (that you trust and feel safe with) if any of them would be interested in developing their abilities or helping you develop yours. Perhaps you have friends who are interested in developing their psychic skills, but don't live near you. For example, you can do exercise 1 over the phone, via emails, or through regular mail, and you could do exercises 2 and 4 via regular mail. Granted, it won't be the same as doing these in person but for those of you without access to a big group of people, there are ways that you can practice. The main thing is that you need people to practice on.

Once you've gathered a group of people interested in developing their psychic skills, I want you to make a commitment to meet every week, same time and same place, if possible, for continuity. It's helpful if you don't all know each other well already, because you're going to be doing readings on each other. Prior knowledge about someone can interfere with whether or not the information you're receiving is real or based on what you already know about them, especially when you're first starting readings.

Remember, it's crucial to choose people you feel safe with and who won't make fun of you. Our egos get in the way enough as it is when it comes to developing these gifts; don't make it harder on yourself by choosing friends that you're going to continually have to *prove yourself* to. That kind of situation can set up a huge block. None of us likes to be made fun of or put on the spot, so make sure you're not sabotaging your development by the people you're choosing to work with.

Turning Your Abilities On and Off

My guess is, if you're reading this book, you are aware of having some kind of psychic abilities, but they are hit or miss. You can't call on them whenever you want to, and they might come when you least expect or want them to. This is very common with untrained psychic abilities, so don't get discouraged. It is possible to turn your abilities on and shut them off at will.

Often my students tell me that once they've gotten their psychic channels opened up, they don't want to shut them down for fear they'll never come back on. I can assure you, they will. In fact, in the beginning, it's just as important to be able to turn your abilities off so you don't develop a "third-eye headache."

When you're just starting, you should only do a couple of exercises a week. Opening up your third eye and/or psychic ears takes time, and it's like exercising any muscle in your body: if you push yourself too hard, you'll hurt yourself. In this case, a third-eye headache feels like a tight band around your forehead, and aspirin isn't going to take it away. The only way to feel better is to shut down psychically and walk away from practicing for a while. The area in the middle of your forehead will always be sensitive, but in the beginning of your development, it will be especially so. Don't push it simply because you're excited. You have plenty of time to develop your abilities...so pace yourself.

I want you to do a simple exercise right now. Close your eyes and focus on the middle of your forehead. Imagine there is a closed eye there, and next to it is a light switch, which is currently in the down or "off" position.

Now imagine turning the light switch "on," and visualize your third eye slowly opening up (yes, it's really there). It may open just a tiny bit or it may open up widely. It will open to some degree.

Now visualize a zipper on the top of your head. Imagine slowly unzipping it.

Now sit and focus on this picture (of an opened third eye and the energy above your head opened up) for about thirty seconds. What does your head feel like? It may be a subtle difference or a very obvious feeling. Just feel it.

Once you've done this, zip the zipper back up and turn off the light switch by your third eye. See your third eye close. Now note what this feels like.

Now go through and do this entire exercise again. Turn on the light switch by your third eye, unzip the zipper on top of your head, experience the sensation of being open psychically for about thirty seconds, and then close down your third eye and the energy on top of your head, noting how you now feel different.

This is all you need to do to open yourself up and close down psychically. You open up your third eye so that you can receive pictures, visions, or images, and by unzipping the zipper on top of your head, you open up your psychic ears so that you can receive messages.

It's important for you to know that you can control your gifts — that you can turn them on and turn them off when you want. It's also important for you to be able to recognize how it feels when they are on or off. This will help you discern between when you're being psychic and when you're having your own thoughts.

The Exercises

I'm going to teach you the same psychic development exercises my teacher taught me thirty-seven years ago. Some of these are going to work better for you than others, but I want you to do all of them several times until you find the ones that work best. Sometimes you might be blocked with one of these exercises, but what I've found is that this usually has more to do with the person you're practicing with than with the exercise itself. If you find you're stuck when doing one of these, try it with a different partner first rather than chuck the whole exercise.

If you have gathered a group of people, you need to pair up, and then every week make sure you have a different partner, so that you don't read the same person every time. As soon as you're all present, count off to determine who your partner will be. This is easiest if the group is an even number. If there are six people in your group, for example, count off to three twice and those people with matching numbers become partners for this week. Likewise, if you have eight people in the group, count to four twice, or ten people, count to five twice. If you have an odd number of people (such as five), create one "pairing" of three people, and have them read each other round-robin style, so that no one reads or is read twice.

Once you have your partner, you can do the exercises in one of two ways:

1) You can take turns with your partner, and as the information comes, you can say it out loud and get feedback as you go, or

2) You can both do the exercise at the same time, each of you writing down all of the information you're receiving on a piece of paper. Then, when you're both finished, you can review each other's paper and give feedback on accuracy.

In either case, whenever you are evaluating the psychic information of your partner, be sure you don't stretch the truth in order to make the information seem true. That's not going to help either of you develop your abilities. The information either fits or it doesn't!

Before You Begin: Opening Up Fully

Here is a more in-depth version of the opening exercise, which you should do before every practice session.

Sit in a chair, close your eyes, and take a few relaxing breaths. Ask your body to release stress and tension as you exhale. Notice any parts of your body that are feeling tight or in pain. When you inhale, visualize your breath going into that body part to bring calmness and ease the pain.

Let your body sink into the chair so that it feels completely supported.

Using your imagination, visualize roots coming out of the bottom of your feet, going down through the floor, and reaching at least six to ten feet into the ground. This will help your body feel grounded while you are opened up psychically.

Now visualize your third eye, located in the middle of your forehead, with the light switch next to it. Visualize turning the light switch to the on position and your third eye slowly opening. Next, visualize the zipper on the top of your head. Unzip the zipper, which in turn opens up your psychic ears.

You have now opened yourself up to Universal Truth. As you develop your abilities, you will become more and more aware of the feeling of this dimension, which is very light.

Next, go to your solar plexus (the area around your belly button), and visualize a white light inside. This is where your intuition resides. Ask God (or if you prefer, Universal Truth or Knowledge) to help you know the truth of the information you receive and to help you accurately interpret the information.

Now all systems are go, and you are ready to do some psychic work. Your third eye is open, you've opened your psychic ears, and you've got your wonderful helper, the inner voice (or intuition), ready to help you interpret the information you're about to receive. Let's begin.

EXERCISE 1
Names

In this exercise, you will practice tuning into a person's vibration by focusing on his or her first name. It's not necessary to have a full name. Have your partner give you the first name of someone he or she knows well. Write the name on a piece of paper, close your eyes, and ask the Universe to give you clear, accurate information about this person. Remember to be respectful of personal boundaries, and ask for information that will help you know that you're on the right track.

Focus on the name. Say it over and over to yourself, either out loud or silently. When a thought or a picture comes into your mind, tell your partner or write it down (depending on how you're conducting the exercise) and then go back to the name. Continue repeating it to yourself. If a picture or thought of someone you know keeps coming into your mind, write down the characteristics you think of when you think of that person.

Now tell your partner or write down the thoughts and images that seem goofy or insignificant. You'll be surprised at how often the information that seems irrelevant is quite relevant. If you start "thinking" about what information you're getting, your intellect can actually block you, so just keep focusing on the name and write down whatever thoughts, pictures, or sensations come to you. Don't worry about being wrong. In the beginning, we just want to get things moving. The human tendency is to complicate matters, so remind yourself to keep it simple and focus on the name. If your head does get in the way, and you start doubting what you're doing and thinking it's a waste of time, remind yourself that you're developing one of your gifts.

In the beginning, spend only about five minutes focusing on the name. When the time is up, or the information stops coming in, run each piece of information by your intuition for validation. It will let you know if the pictures, thoughts, or feelings are accurate.

For example, let's say that these are some of the things that came to you about the person: outgoing, picture of a sports car, mother, blue dress, pumpkins, Johnny Mathis. Take one item at a time and focus on your intuition, asking it if the information is relevant. Each time, you will get an inner knowing of either yes, no, or maybe.

Outgoing? *Yes*

A sports car? *Yes, but there's an odd feeling with it, like we don't have all the information*

Mother? *Yes*

Blue dress? *No*

Pumpkins? *Yes*

Johnny Mathis? *Yes*

Now go back to the sports car and ask for clarity. Ask questions like: Does the person have a sports car? *No.* Does the person want a sports car? *Yes.*

After you've checked out all the information intuitively, and feel satisfied with your answers, give your partner your list and get his or her feedback.

If none of the information is accurate, don't get discouraged. At first, the main goal is simply to get your psychic centers opened up and get the pictures and thoughts coming to you. We'll work a lot on accuracy later, so for now be patient and stay with it. The difficulty might have been with the name you were given, so ask your partner for another name and try again.

After you've finished, ask the Universe to clear you psychically.

Let's talk through another example. Let's say this time your partner gives you the name "Tom," but you happen to have a brother (or husband, cousin, or friend) with the same name, and you can't get past thinking about your relative. Ask your partner for the first initial of Tom's last name (let's say it's "T"), but only the first initial. This is important for a couple of reasons. One is that when we focus on a person's first name, we can usually tap into his or her energy without much problem, so it's not necessary to know last names. In addition, not providing a last name protects the person's anonymity. And last, sometimes names can throw us off. If we know the person's last name is, say, Goldstein, we might immediately assume the person is Jewish and start thinking of common Jewish characteristics or stereotypes. That's not being psychic. That's called playing it safe. Our mind (and ego) plays all kinds of tricks on us in order not to be wrong, but this gets in the way of hearing the truth about a person. That's why I always tell my students to stay away from people's last names and just stick with first names if possible.

Now, getting back to "Tom T." As before, focus all your attention on the name. When your mind starts to wander, come back to the name and repeat it over and over to yourself: Tom T., Tom T., Tom T. Soon, images (clairvoyance), thoughts (clairaudience), and feelings (clairsentience) will start to come. When they do, tell your partner or write them down: Airplanes. Computers. Gray suit. Blueberries. Wedding band. You might get a feeling of far away.

Notice if your emotions change over the course of the exercise. While repeating Tom's name, do you find yourself feeling angry, sad, happy, melancholy, fearful? Write down any noticeable changes in your emotions or your physical body while focusing on his name. If you're a strong clairsentient, you may pick up through your body that the person has physical problems (if Tom has kidney problems, your lower back might suddenly start to hurt). When the images, thoughts, and feelings stop, run the list by your intuition for accuracy.

Airplane? *Yes*

Computers? *Yes*

Gray suit? *Yes*

Blueberries? *Yes*

Wedding band? *No*

Far away? *Yes*

Now let's take this a step further. Go down the list again, and ask each item for more clarification.

Airplane: Does he own a plane? *No.* Does he fly airplanes? *No.* Does he travel a lot by airplane? *Yes.* Is there anything else significant about airplanes? *No.*

Computer: Is he a computer programmer? *No.* Does he work with computers? *Yes.*

Gray suit: Is there any significance to the gray suit other than that he wears one? *No.*

Blueberries: Does he like blueberries? *Yes.* Is there more significance here? *Yes.* Does he grow them? *Yes.* Is there more significance? *No.*

Wedding band: No thoughts, feelings, or visions come when you say the words *wedding band,* so let it go and move on.

Far away: Does he live far away? *Yes and no.* Hmm. Okay. Pin it down. Does he live in more than one place? *Yes.* Is one of them far away? *Yes.* Is there anything more significant than that? *No.*

When you feel satisfied with your answers, hand them to your partner for verification. Remember that you're in the beginning stages of understanding how all of this works, so look at every situation as a tool for learning. Pay as much attention to the possible sources of wrong information as to being excited over the information you get right. And again, be honest with each other regarding accuracy. Real psychic information will not be fuzzy or sort of correct, so don't stretch to make the information fit if it really doesn't. Don't spare each other's feelings. That's not going to help you develop.

And again, before moving on to another exercise, ask the Universe to clear you psychically. You may need to ask two or three times to make sure you are cleared of that person's energy. Whenever there is a lot of information and I can't seem to disconnect from a particular person, I imagine I have an eraser in my hand and I literally wipe off the area of my third eye. It works well.

When You Finish: Closing Up

When you're finished doing your practice exercises, you need to not only clear yourself of the people you've been reading, but you need to shut down psychically. Do the following after every session, which is a combination of the closing visualizations described under "Controlling Your Abilities" above and the clearing meditation described under "Protecting Yourself Psychically" in chapter 2.

Close your physical eyes, take a couple of deep relaxing breaths, and release any tension that might be sitting in your body. Visualize the light switch by your third eye, which is on right now. Imagine switching it off, and your third eye closing. Then visualize zipping up the top of your head.

Now ask the Universe or God to please clear you:

Please clear my body
Clear my body
Please clear my mind
Clear my mind
Please clear my soul
Clear my soul
Please clear me psychically
Clear me psychically

It's very important to do this clearing exercise because you don't want to carry any of the people you've just read around with you. Take a couple of relaxing breaths and open your eyes when you feel refreshed. Now you're back in this reality and can go about your everyday business. If you still feel somewhat spacey, again ask the Universe to clear you, and then ground yourself further by doing one or several of the suggestions listed under "Grounding" in chapter 4.

EXERCISE 2
Photographs

In this exercise, you will read photographs *without* looking at them. To begin, get three to four photographs of people you know well, and one of them can be of you. Each photo should be of only one person, and preferably without any pets in the picture; pets have their own personalities, which can cause confusion when trying to read the picture. Put each photo in an envelope and mark the outside with the person's initials so that you will know whose picture you have given to your partner. Finally, exchange pictures one at a time with your partner, making sure the photo isn't visible through the envelope; if it is, give them the envelope with the photograph facing down. For the first photo, you can tell your partner the person's sex, but that's all I want you to share with them.

Decide if you want to go one at a time, or both read the photos at the same time. If you choose to go one at a time, decide who is going to work first, and, as the information comes to that person, tell your partner out loud what you're getting or writing down on a tablet and hand it to them when you are finished. If you decide to work at the same time, simply write down all your information and exchange these notes when you are both finished writing. If you are in a group of three, each one in the group should pass a photograph to the person on their right, and then everyone should read the photos at the same time. As in Exercise 1, begin by doing the opening up visualizations: open your third eye, your psychic ears, and your intuition.

Then, hold the envelope containing the photo in your hand, and ask the Universe, God, and your spirit guides to give you clear, accurate information about this person. Spend about five minutes on this. Write down everything that comes to you, no matter how silly or insignificant it seems. When it feels like there's no more information coming (but don't go much longer than five minutes), run the list by your intuition for accuracy. Don't get frustrated in the beginning if this seems tedious or time-consuming. It will become second nature after a while. When you've finished checking with your intuition, you and your partner should exchange lists and then give each other honest feedback about your accuracy.

Once you've finished the reading and gotten feedback, then you can both look at the pictures. You might be surprised at how the person you read looks because it may be very different than what you saw in your third eye. Our minds are always working, and your mind may have put together a composite sketch based on random information you were picking up. Don't be alarmed if the picture you had in your head looks different than the actual person. Focus more on your list of attributes and discuss them with your partner. Work with each other. Share any information that would help your partner understand the images, thoughts, and feelings he or she got.

When you've finished discussing your readings, ask the Universe to clear you of the person's energy. Then do the next picture, except this time I want you to give your partner the first name of the person in the photograph. I want you to see the difference it makes when you have the person's name also.

You may find that you are very accurate with the first picture, but not so accurate with the second one, and this could be for a couple of reasons:

1) The person you read isn't that easy to read.

2) Your ego got in the way, wanting to make sure you were right the second time also.

If you don't get it right, don't be too hard on yourself. This is all very normal. You will go through various stages of being nervous, wanting to be right, feeling afraid when you are right, and yet worrying about being wrong. We go through a lot of changes as we develop our abilities, which is another reason why I want you to keep a journal. Write out all your thoughts and feelings about your psychic abilities — your frustrations, excitement, anxiety, fears, and goals. Also, if you're aware of any blocks, write those down, too. This is definitely a journey, and it's going to take some time to "get there." Try to enjoy every step along the way.

EXERCISE 3
Billets

Remember Johnny Carson's character "Carnac the Magnificent"? The turbaned fortune teller who would hold up to his third eye a piece of paper with a hidden question written on it and tell you the answer? Those pieces of paper with questions on them are called *billets*.

Back in the sixties and seventies, there were billet readers who would hold sessions for the public to come and get psychic advice. These were usually held in a large convention room or church. I attended several, and they went like this: you'd go in, pay your five dollars, and get a piece of paper to write a question on. You were supposed to address the billet to one of your deceased relatives or spirit guides, ask them a question about your life, and sign it in a loving way. You were to hold the billet for about thirty seconds while thinking about your question, just in case there were a couple of questions you were thinking of asking. Then you would fold it twice to make sure the billet reader couldn't possibly read your question, and someone would come along with a basket (like the collection plate at church) to gather them all and take them to the reader standing at the podium. An assistant would put cotton balls on the reader's eyes, followed by a blindfold. Then for the next couple of hours, the reader would reach into the basket and take out a billet, hold it up to his or her third eye, and proceed to give the answer out loud.

The reader would always say something to help the crowd distinguish whose question it was by saying something like, "This question is for someone on the right side of the room whose first name starts with an F. You wrote this to your sister in spirit, and she says to tell you that the answer to your question is that you have to be patient until springtime and then you will get the guidance you are praying for." The reader was oftentimes more specific in his or her answers, but you never knew what to expect. Sometimes the person would say something like, "This billet was written by a person on the left side of the room who was going to wear a red sweater today, but changed their mind at the last minute." And then she or he would proceed to give the answer.

Never once did the reader look at a question, but the skeptics all said billet readers had hidden microphones and tiny mirrors inside the blindfolds, and that's how they knew who was in the crowd (oh brother!).

Now, it's your turn. I want you to do billets with your partner. Both of you take a piece of paper and write a question to one of your guides or a deceased relative. The question can be anything that you would like advice about. Then thank the person for helping you and sign it, just as if you had written a letter. For example:

Dear Grandma:
I'm thinking about applying for a job at the saw mill. Do you think this is a wise move, and can you tell me a good time to do this? Thank you.
Love, Jake

Fold the piece of paper twice and hold it in your hands for about thirty seconds while you focus on your question. After you've both done this, exchange billets.

Before trying to psychically read the billets, make sure you both do the opening up exercises described above under "Before You Begin: Opening Up Fully." Then, without looking at the billets, close your eyes and either hold the billet up to your third eye, like Johnny Carson, or hold the billet in your hands and simply focus your attention on it. Ask God or your guides to help you bring through clear, accurate information that will help answer this person's question. As images, thoughts, and feelings start coming, write them down, either on the outside of the billet or on a separate piece of paper. Every time the information stops coming, ask if there's more information for this question.

Students sometimes groan about billets, but this is their ego talking. They feel like they don't have any control over the outcome of the reading since they don't know what the question is. Actually, *not* knowing the question is what makes this such a good exercise, since it trains you in how to be an open channel for information.

Write down everything that comes to you. Don't assume anything is stupid or insignificant. Remember, the only way to learn is to pay attention to everything. It's trial and error at first. Whether you get it right or get it wrong, always learn from it!

Remember, too, to work with your partner. Don't play *stump the psychic* by trying to trick your partner with fake or insignificant questions. You're in this together. Ask authentic questions in the billets and give honest feedback about the answers. When you're finished with one billet, be sure to clear yourself before doing another one.

If the answer your partner gives you in response to your question just doesn't seem to fit, two things might be going on.

1) If there were two questions you were thinking of writing, the answer you got may apply to the other question you were going to ask.

2) It could simply mean your partner didn't get accurate information.

In the beginning of doing these exercises, I suggest only doing a couple per session. You can work up to doing more, but remember, this is a process, and you don't want a third-eye headache. When you've decided you're done doing billets for the day, do the closing exercise described above under "When You Finish: Closing Up."

EXERCISE 4
Psychometry

A lot of psychics do psychometry. This is holding and reading a personal object, such as jewelry, clothing, or a favorite toy. Everything we have and use — our clothing and furniture, our offices and bedrooms, our cars and toys, and especially our jewelry — have our vibes in them. When psychics read an object, metal is preferred because it holds people's energy or vibes longer than anything else. Many psychics who work with the police trying to locate a missing person use psychometry.

For this next exercise, I want you to bring a couple pieces of jewelry for your partner to read. One piece can be yours, but the others need to belong to a friend or relative you know well. Avoid antique jewelry if at all possible. Secondhand jewelry can be difficult to read because it has more than one person's vibes in it, which will make it difficult to verify the information that you receive.

Incidentally, if you are someone who loves antique jewelry, I would suggest saging it after you purchase it. Burn some sage and hold the object in the smoke for a few minutes, asking the Universe to clear it of all the vibes it's holding. This is especially important for psychic people because we're ultrasensitive to begin with, and wearing someone else's vibes all day can actually drain our energy. I also suggest saging a new piece of jewelry simply because a lot of people may have handled it before you bought it.

Before starting the exercise, open up psychically using the visualization described above under "Before You Begin: Opening Up Fully."

When you've finished, exchange a single piece of jewelry with your partner. Hold the jewelry in your hands and close your eyes. Ask the piece of jewelry to tell you what information it's holding about the person who wears it. As the information starts to come, write it down on a piece of paper. Remember not to censor the information no matter how stupid or insignificant it may seem. Just let it flow to you. If your ego gets in the way and you start worrying about being wrong, remind yourself that it's okay to make mistakes and that this is how you learn to discern between significant and insignificant information.

When you feel done receiving information, run everything by your intuition for validation, and then share the information with your partner. Be sure to give each other honest feedback. Remember to clear yourself before moving on to another piece of jewelry. When you are finished with the psychometry exercises, be sure to shut down psychically using the closing exercises above under "When You Finish: Closing Up."

ASKING QUESTIONS

Remember Columbo, the inquisitive TV detective played by Peter Falk who is always driving people crazy with his countless questions? Well, sometimes when we're trying to get psychic information, we need to do the same thing. We need to put on our "Columbo coat" and ask the Universe a lot of questions in order to get the information rolling in.

Here's a list of suggested questions I put together for my students so that instead of just waiting for information to come, they can go after it. You should do the same thing when doing these four exercises: Don't sit in absolute silence patiently waiting and waiting — ask questions! You can add your own questions to this list, but remember to always be respectful of people's boundaries. Don't ask questions that would breach anyone's privacy.

You can ask:

Is the person male or female?

How tall is the person? Under five feet or over six feet?

How old is the person? Under twenty or over thirty? Youthful, middle aged, or old?

Does the person have a petite build, a medium build, or a heavy build?

Does the person have light hair or dark hair? Blonde, brown, black, or red?

What is the person's eye color? Brown, green, blue, or hazel?

Does the person have any distinguishing features, such as eyeglasses, a beard or mustache, moles, freckles, or scars?

Does the person have any health issues? (Notice your own body while tuning in. Do any parts hurt?)

What is the person's marital status: married, single, divorced, or widowed? (Note: If the person is living with someone, it will come up as married.)

Does the person have any children? How many and what sex?

Is the person living or deceased? (Note: A deceased person's energy still feels alive, but it usually seems far away.)

What is the person's profession?

Does the person have any hobbies?

Does the person play a musical instrument or have any artistic abilities?

Does the person belong to an organized religion or follow a spiritual practice, or is he or she atheist?

Then there are dozens of questions you can ask about a person's personality:

Is the person gentle or aggressive?

Is the person introverted or extroverted?

Is the person pessimistic or optimistic?

Is the person generally cautious or a risk-taker?

Is the person openly affectionate or reserved?

Is the person moody or does he or she have an even temperament?

Is the person serious or does he or she have a lively sense of humor?

Is the person most often a leader or a follower?

Is the person reliable and consistent or unreliable and inconsistent?
Does the person guard his or her privacy or is the person open?
Is the person more of an intellectual type or a creative type?

And finally, when you've run out of specific questions, don't forget to simply ask if there is any more information your guides can provide.

Chapter 7

Where Do You Go from Here?
Continuing Your Psychic Development

I once got an email from a woman who said she had a week's vacation coming up and wanted to know if I would teach her and her niece how to develop their psychic abilities. Needless to say, I was a little flabbergasted by her request. Psychic development takes *years* of practice, not weeks.

If you've ever seen John Edward or James Van Praagh on television, you've probably noticed that both of them humbly say that anyone can do what they do. What is rarely mentioned is how long it took each of them to develop their gifts and how and what they did to get to the level that they're at today. Indeed, as they will tell you in their books, it took them both many years of practice to understand and fine-tune their gifts.

If your goal is to become a professional psychic, remember that there are many important things you have to learn and master — on a personal as well as a psychic level — in order for you to achieve that goal: interpretation, how to work with people, learning how to hear your guides, developing accuracy, taking good care of yourself physically, staying grounded in this reality and maintaining normalcy, finding a balance between living in this dimension and being open to the other dimensions or realities, learning how to control your gifts so you're not overly sensitive to the world around you.

Developing your abilities is a natural process. It is a journey along which you will gain much wisdom. Don't try to hurry it along or take shortcuts. Consider whatever you're going through right now as exactly what you should be going through, and when you're ready for the next stage of development, it will arrive. Trust me.

Meditation and Reading

On the days when you're not practicing the exercises, I want you to spend a minimum of five minutes sitting in silence, meditating and focusing on the white light deep inside in the area of your solar plexus. This is a good discipline to learn for anyone. While you're focusing on the light, feel the calmness and safety of this light and the wisdom within it. If your mind wanders, keep coming back to the light.

When sitting in silence, you can ask your guides to make themselves known to you. Ask if they have any direction or guidance for you regarding your life. Ask God to reveal himself/herself to you. If your mind starts to wander, refocus on the white light.

As you get more comfortable meditating, extend the time. The longer you spend in silent communication with your inner voice (God) and your guides, the stronger the connection will become. As you continue to grow spiritually, you'll want to spend more time meditating on the light, and I encourage you to do so. This is one of the best ways for us to establish conscious contact with God.

Is the Silence Too Quiet for You?

If you find you have a difficult time sitting and concentrating in silence, that doesn't mean meditation isn't for you. If you prefer having some background noise, go ahead and create whatever environment makes you most comfortable. Don't hassle yourself about it. My brother Michael usually has some kind of background noise, like a stereo or TV playing low, when he meditates or does psychic readings because he says distractions help him hear spirits easier. I once had a student who always sat by the classroom's air conditioner, which hummed, because silence was too much of a distraction for her when she was doing the exercises. Experiment and see what way works best for you.

Besides doing the exercises in this book and meditating each day, you can also keep reading about psychics and psychic development. I just want to caution you about getting too much information too fast. This can keep you stuck in your intellect, and it can lead you to expect perfectionism; both are counterproductive. In fact, when you read something is as important as what you read. Select authors you have heard of and trust, then evaluate whether the timing is right for you to read them. An important rule of thumb when picking out the right books for your needs is to run them by your intuition. Your intuition knows what your needs are and where you're at in your psychic development, and it will guide you to the books you're ready for next. It'll never steer you wrong. See the end of this book for a short list of recommended books and audiocassettes.

Upgrades: Your Level of Development Continually Changes

The three most important keys to your development are patience, practice, and honoring the process. On the other hand, I also want to encourage you not to be satisfied with the level you've grown to. Throughout my years as a psychic, I've never stayed at the same level for more than two years. As I continually open myself up to what's possible, my psychic gifts have continued to develop to a much deeper level. If you stick with it, your gifts will grow, too.

In the beginning, I did five-minute readings for friends. Over time, I was able to do fifteen-minute readings. Then they stretched out to thirty minutes, and now my readings run forty-five minutes to an hour.

When I got on my spiritual path and started developing my relationship with God, the readings changed again. Deeper information started coming through. When I worked on my own emotional issues through therapy and twelve-step programs, I was able to channel information that helped people in their own emotional healing. As I got my own health in order, I started reading other people's health more clearly. When I started working with my own soul through hypnosis, my mind opened up to the possibilities of working with people's souls, and the readings became more meaningful for their life's purpose.

One of my students once called this process getting an "upgrade," and I get such a kick out of this term because it's such a perfect way to describe these periods we go through in our development when we're about to progress to a new level. You'll find from time to time that you are completely shut down psychically. The image that just came to me as I was typing this was of a water tower with an enormous tarp thrown over it that I drove by the other day. It was undergoing repairs, and when you go through these periods, you will feel like someone has put a tarp on your abilities and you're *under construction,* so to speak. When this happens, there is an internal shift going on with your third eye and psychic ears, and no matter how much you want to use or practice your abilities, you won't be able to. During these down times, when you're getting the latest revisions to your software, you're going to have to mentally hang a "closed for business" sign on yourself. When you're in one of these periods, stay busy with your life. Go to movies. Work in the yard. Hang out with friends. Go for walks. Do things that make your body feel grounded. Clean your closets. Do all those things you've been putting off while developing your psychic abilities.

I wish I could tell you scientifically what's going on with our "psychic parts" when we're shut down, but I can't. I can assure you that when your gifts open up again, they'll be stronger and you'll definitely feel "upgraded."

You'll also notice that your abilities might shut off when you're going through a tough time emotionally or there is some kind of challenge that you're facing. Our abilities shut down as a way to protect us from too much coming at us on a psychic level. Be patient and just know that your gifts will open back up when you're ready for them.

The Possibilities Are Endless

Opening up your third eye and psychic ears and being tuned into your intuition throughout the day will create endless possibilities in your life.

You'll communicate with God throughout the day. You will get helpful guidance from your spirit guides. You will see heaven while standing in your kitchen and be able to communicate with your deceased loved ones.

You will be able to see aliens if you want and be aware of other solar systems. You'll communicate with others through mental telepathy as much if not more than you do verbally. You'll be able to do remote viewing if you choose. You may see auras. You'll be able to see sickness in people before they're even aware of it. You'll be able to see your own future, once you learn how to be emotionally detached.

There are so many possible ways that your gifts may manifest themselves. Here are four areas that I'd like to cover in more depth: reading past lives, communicating with the dead, ghostbusting, and finding missing people.

Reading Past Lives

I'll never forget the first time I got a picture of a past life. I must have stared at those pictures for a good two to three minutes while my mind struggled to accept what I was seeing. At that point in my psychic development, I didn't believe in reincarnation, so my intellect was trying to come up with every possible interpretation of the pictures other than that they represented a past life.

A friend had asked me to tune into her relationship with her boyfriend and see if I could get any information that would help her understand why they had so many problems. She also wanted to know what she could do to resolve their conflicts.

The first picture that came was an old-time doctor's office, and I saw a woman in a nurse's uniform. Even though this nurse didn't look like my friend, I knew on a psychic level that this was her. The next picture was a drunken doctor, passed out at his desk, followed by a picture of her covering for him with patients all the time. I could see she had a love/hate relationship with him. My guides said she loved him but hated his drinking, and that she'd search his office and home every day for whiskey bottles and then pour them out.

The part that was so disturbing to me was that all these images looked like they were set in the 1800s. Since I didn't want to entertain thoughts of reincarnation, my mind became increasingly preoccupied with trying to find some more "rational" explanation. At some point, my guides told me to just relax and open up to the information. They said I could deal with my own feelings of disbelief later, but that for now I needed to give my friend this information because it would help her know how to resolve their major conflicts. I decided to take their advice and set my "stuff" aside so that the guides could continue passing on more information.

They said that my friend had been very judgmental of her boyfriend's alcoholism in their previous lifetime, which is why she was an alcoholic in this lifetime. The other big issue was that she was always taking care of him, and he didn't want to be taken care of. He, too, was in recovery from alcoholism in this lifetime, and he wanted to be on his own, but she mothered him to the point of smothering him, never feeling that he could do anything on his own. She got her self-worth by feeling needed, and she didn't want to give it up. She had a lot of resentments toward him that she didn't understand and was always feeling like he never appreciated "all I've done for you." Every time he gained more independence from her, she resented him even more.

After this, the guides gave my friend some great suggestions as to how she and her boyfriend could resolve their conflicts, and the experience really opened my eyes to the truth of reincarnation, which I soon came to believe in. Since then, I've seen many past lives, and it's likely that at some point you will get past-life information, whether you accept reincarnation or not, and you need to understand how to identify it.

The pictures will not look modern, and they may *feel* very old as well, as if your guides are drawing you back in time. You might also get an old musty smell, which will indicate that what you are seeing occurred a time long ago.

In time, you will come to recognize past-life pictures immediately. Sometimes your guides will give you the dates automatically, and sometimes you'll have to ask for them. You can ask the location of the past life, and you can ask your guides to identify the people in the pictures. The images usually only show the key people that you are dealing with in this lifetime. Sometimes your guides may feel it's best for the person not to know who he or she was in a previous lifetime, and they won't share that information. Go ahead and ask all the questions you want, but remember your guides have the final say as far as what information the person can handle knowing.

Communicating with the Dead

As you develop your abilities, you may find your gift is manifesting through mediumship, or communicating with people's deceased loved ones. This happened to my sister, Nikki. She was channeling healings to people, and slowly, one by one, people's deceased relatives started showing up in her healing room. At first she didn't know what to do because the person hadn't expressed any desire to hear from his or her deceased relatives, but she decided to relay their messages anyway. She soon realized the messages were very meaningful to people, and that bringing through these messages was part of their healing, so she now uses her gifts in this way as well.

If this happens to you, don't be naïve about it. Not every spirit who claims to be someone's deceased loved one is telling the truth. I've seen earthbound spirits try to mess with people in this way, so you need to be discerning and firm. Simply tell the spirit you want some kind of proof that will validate the spirit's identity. Then, when the spirit gives you a message, don't censor or edit it, but pass it along as accurately as possible so the client can evaluate its authenticity. If someone came through a medium claiming to be my father and gave me a message in a very eloquent manner — like "Hello, I am Echo's father. Please tell my loving daughter that I am very proud of all her work." — I would be suspicious because my dad doesn't talk like that. My father's message would sound more like, "Hey babe, this is your ol' man. Keep up the good work."

If you are channeling a deceased loved one, be very precise in relaying the language of the message, and then confirm with your friend or client that the person sounds correct. If your client still isn't sure, ask the spirit to give you some concrete evidence of who they are. Don't accept generalities; tell them you want specifics. And if you come to believe the message isn't authentic, get rid of the earthbound spirit by telling them to move on into the light.

Also remember that our appearance changes when we go over to the other side. As soon as we die, our souls usually start to look younger. For instance, if someone's father had gray hair when he passed over, but had black hair when he was younger, his soul may now appear to you psychically to have black hair. If he was quite overweight when he died, he probably won't be looking like that now because he's no longer living in that overweight body. He is now simply energy. If you'd like to know more about the soul after it leaves the physical body, check out my book *Echoes of the Soul.* This will give you a lot of helpful information regarding the soul's perspective on life, death, life after death, and heaven.

Ghostbusting

One of the "perks" of developing your third eye is that at some point you'll begin to see spirits and other dimensions. Usually at first you will just see little white lights, similar to fireflies, out of the corners of your eyes. Over time, and this could take years, you will start to see "blobs of energy." Gradually these will become more pronounced forms of energy similar to a human form. You might see half of them at first, or you might see fully materialized spirits. Eventually you'll learn to distinguish between spirits, angels, guides, and earthbound spirits or ghosts. It's been my experience that if your gift is to clear homes and businesses of these earthbound spirits or ghosts, you'll be able to tune into them quite easily.

Teaching you how to clear homes of unwanted spirits takes a lot more than a couple pages of information, so if this is something you're feeling called to do, I would definitely suggest getting a copy of my books *Relax, It's Only a Ghost* and *Dear Echo*. The whole topic of ghosts is covered extensively in both books.

Finding Missing People

My students often tell me that they are interested in developing their abilities mainly so that they can help the police find missing children. If this is something you're hoping to do with your gifts, there are some things you need to know.

The irony of wanting to find missing people (especially children) is that we're doing it because we care, and yet in order to be an effective instrument for information, we have to completely detach our emotions to the point where we don't care what we see. In other words, we have to go in with our psychic eyes and ears open and our hearts on hold. If you go in with your heart wide open, wanting to find someone *really badly,* you've lost your objectivity, and your caring is going to block any "negative" information from coming in.

What you have to do is *detach* your emotions and stay that way. Get the person's name and work with that as long as possible before bringing in other things to read like photographs or material possessions. Something as simple as a toy or an adorable picture of the child will open up your emotions, and your objectivity will go out the window.

If the missing person's relatives or friends have called on your assistance, tell them to keep the details to a minimum. Ask them not to "lavish" you with the whole story until *after* you've given them all the information you can get. People want to share all that they can, but you need to walk a fine line: the more you know about the missing person's circumstances, or of the fears of the missing person's family, the harder it will be for you to maintain the emotional distance you need to receive the information.

Working with the police

So often when there's a child missing in the news, my students will try to locate the girl or boy. They will get bits and pieces of information, like a shallow grave or a tree next to a hill. Maybe they will see the name of a town, but not the state. They might get an image of a child still alive and frightened, or they may get an image of a murder. My students become so anxious to tell the police what they've seen, and I understand their enthusiasm because I've felt it myself many times, but — and this is a big but:

Unless you have concrete information, like the name of the town and the state, the name of the hill, the name of the street the house is on, the exact location where the body is buried, and so on, the police are not going to be interested in your information.

I once kept having the same visions over and over of a missing child near where I live in Minnesota, and the policeman I called said that he really wanted to help me out — and I believe he was sincere — but that he didn't have the manpower to chase down every hunch or vision that psychics get. He told me that if I really thought I knew where this kid was, I should go look for him myself and then call if I found something concrete. Given the intense interest missing person cases can draw, it's a sad truth that the police are not always equipped to handle all the information they receive.

The other problem you will run into is that a lot of police officers think that psychics are frauds. Not all think this, but a lot do. The police, in general, are not going to welcome your psychic impressions with open arms. They will be very skeptical if you show up unasked at the precinct — and they should be. Until you prove otherwise, they have no reason not to think that you aren't some "whacko" taking advantage of the situation just to get attention. If you want them to take you seriously, you need to present them with verifiable, hard evidence, some kind of proof that you know what you're talking about.

I'm not trying to burst the bubble of anyone who is feeling called to do this kind of work, but you need to know the reality of how it can go. I've also worked with members of the police force who were very nice and tried working with the sketchy pieces of information I've given them. But even when the police encourage your participation, it's very hard to get the sort of information needed to locate the child.

The work itself is very difficult, and I only do it if a family member asks me to. It's not easy to detach your emotions and push away all the information we're fed from the media. So often psychics immediately get the idea that the person is dead because that's what we see so often in the news.

I remember a few years ago a dear friend called in a panic because her granddaughter had been missing for a day. My psychic sense was that the girl was with her boyfriend, who was someone her parents didn't know anything about, but my intellect struggled with that information because another local teen had gone missing about a week before and been found murdered. I was praying for the truth of the situation to be revealed to me, but I wasn't trusting the pictures or thoughts coming in. As it turned out, the young girl was with her new boyfriend and she was fine.

If you are asked to find a missing person, my best advice is to get just the name and age of the missing person. Then go off in a room by yourself, ask the Universe to clear you of all preconceived ideas and fears — itself a tall order — and then ask the Universe to give you clear, precise information that will help you find that person. If you get a picture of a hill, ask if there's anything around it that will help locate it. If you get the name of a town, ask for the state. Ask questions of your pictures. Now you must become every inch the detective and get as much information as you can, *but* — and this is another big but:

Only go after the information if someone asks you to or if you know someone in law enforcement who will take you seriously. Otherwise, you'll be sitting with a lot of possibly valuable information and nowhere to go with it.

Chapter 8

Some Final Advice and Cautions

If you are new to psychic phenomenon and just discovering your own abilities, I want to caution you about something that I think is pretty common, and that's going from one extreme to another. My mom and I went through it, and I've seen some of my students go through it. I remember in the beginning of my and my mother's development, we thought that every light that flickered or odd noise the house made was some kind of communication from the spirit world. We bought a Ouija board thinking that that would hasten our psychic development. We read whatever we could find about "the occult," which is what it was called back in the sixties! We went from one end of the pendulum to the other, from having no involvement in any of this at all to totally immersing ourselves in it.

However, this can lead you to burn out quickly, and in a few cases I've watched as frustrated students decided to completely close the door on their abilities. My advice is take it slow and get into all of this in moderation. Continue to live your life the way you were before getting into psychic development. Maintain a balance in your life so that you don't burn out. Ultimately, developing your psychic abilities is about being on a spiritual journey and developing your spiritual gifts. It is about a way of living and seeing, and you must remember to stay grounded in your physical life here on Earth.

Proving Yourself

For as long as I can remember, the once-famous magician James Randi has made his living as a professional skeptic and has put his energies into trying to prove that all psychics are frauds. He is constantly challenging psychics, and he claims to keep a check in his wallet for a large amount of money that he will sign over to the first psychic who can pass a series of tests. I'm not sure what his tests are, but his point is obvious: he doesn't think he'll ever have to cash the check because there aren't any authentic psychics.

This guy knows exactly what he's doing. He's challenging egos, and that's a no-win situation for anyone. Psychics take on his challenge no doubt badly wanting to show him a thing or two; they want to prove they're legitimate while embarrassing Randi, and they probably wouldn't mind the money. But the whole thing is a setup, and the magician knows it. If psychics become focused on winning a competitive ego contest, they will block themselves from being able to use their gifts properly. Most psychics know better than to get into "prove it to me" contests with skeptics like Randi. In part, it's inherently a no-win situation, but also skeptics take great pride in being skeptical, and there's little a psychic can do to convince them of his or her authenticity.

Be careful if you ever hear yourself thinking, "I'll show so and so that I can do this," or "Just wait and see how good I am." This means your ego is in the driver's seat, and most likely your gifts will "fail" you just when you think you need them most. There are lots of James Randis in the world, and oftentimes our egos are quick to rise to our defense, but you need to remind yourself that you don't need to prove anything to anyone. Skeptics will see only what they want to see anyway. If you can avoid this kind of situation, do.

We're Not Fortune Cookies

Another trap that you can sometimes fall into is giving people only the information they want to hear. Some people will come to you only wanting validation or reassurance that everything is okay, and you need to be careful that you're not influenced by this. Don't turn into one of these psychics who just gives people what they want. We're not fortune cookies. We're not supposed to spit out happy predictions for people so that they feel better.

I got a phone call recently from a friend whose boyfriend had just broken up with her, and she wanted me to tell her that they were going to get back together and when. Would he call her and how soon? What was he thinking right now? Did he miss her? Did he regret breaking up?

The timing of her call was so amazing I almost started to laugh: I was in the middle of writing this advice on not giving people what they want just to make them feel better. An image of a stormy road ahead came into my third eye, and I quickly shut it down. I didn't want any more information on the woman's problem because she wasn't asking for the truth, she was asking me to make her feel better.

People will try to manipulate the information you give them by the way they ask their questions: "I applied for this job and I really really want it. Do you see me getting it?" "I met this guy the other night and I really want him to call me. Is he going to and when?" "I felt a lump under my arm the other day but I'm sure it's nothing. You don't think it's anything serious, do you?" "I just invested my life savings on a stock that my cousin says is a sure thing. Do you see me making a fortune?" "I've been trying to get pregnant for four years and nothing's happening. I really want to have a baby. When do you see me getting pregnant?"

When we use our gifts to get information about other people's lives, we don't just get the positive, happy, joyful information. We open up to all of it. Sometimes students will say that they only want to bring through positive information, but as psychics we're not supposed to screen the information we give. When I fell into a bad habit of doing this once, an old psychic friend reminded me that the information doesn't come for my benefit. It comes for the person I'm reading, and I have an obligation to give the person whatever information I receive. It is not mine to decide what the person can and cannot handle.

It can be really tough to deliver "negative" information. An expectant mother might ask about her unborn child, and you might get that the child has some kind of handicap, or will not make it to full term. A client may ask if his spouse is cheating on him, hoping that you'll say no, but you may see that, yes, the spouse is cheating. You might even get the name of the person his wife is having the affair with, and it could turn out to be the person's best friend. A client might ask about her business, saying that she's having some problems and wants to know when things will turn around. You might get an image of the person filing bankruptcy and losing everything. Another client might ask about a lump she can feel in her breast, and you see that it's cancer.

I eventually found a way to head off situations where a client is overly hopeful or even dependent on getting positive answers. When a client asks a very serious question like the ones above, I ask the person if he or she is open to receiving *whatever* information I get. I put it back on the client. If the person says yes, he or she is open to hearing whatever I have to say, then I proceed with the reading and give the person what I get.

You might think that if a client asks a question like the ones listed above, then he or she must want to know the truth of the situation, but I have found that's not always the case. Sometimes the client will say, "No, I don't want to hear *whatever* you have to say. I just want you to reassure me that my spouse isn't having an affair, or that my business isn't going to go bankrupt, or that I don't have cancer." Sometimes when I tell a client that I might not get the information he or she is hoping for, the client withdraws the question.

Something else I've found is that if a client tells me to go ahead and give whatever information I get, and it turns out that the information is "negative," the client usually knows it on a subconscious level and isn't surprised.

If I get information that could be disturbing, I always double-check it with my guides before saying anything. Did I interpret it accurately?

Is there anything I'm missing? I am always very careful because I don't want to misinterpret anything and thereby give false hope or false fear.

Remember, if a person asks a question that could have a painful answer, ask the person if he or she is open to hearing *whatever* comes. You'll be surprised how many people want to hear only good things so that they can feel better. It may be human nature, but it's not a psychic's job.

Avoiding Dependency

You also need to watch out for people who become dependent on your abilities. Some people have no concept of their intuition, and they are continually seeking direction and answers from outside of themselves. You need to set a limit as to how often you think someone should be getting a reading from you and stick to it (unless or until your intuition tells you something different). Most of my clients will call one or two times a year; only once in a while will I get someone who wants a reading more often. I can feel when a client is becoming dependent on the readings to live his or her life, and I immediately discourage it.

I believe this is part of what the Bible is talking about when it warns against "fortune tellers." People should not become dependent on psychics to guide them, they should rely on God, and I agree with that. I think there's a fine line between helping people and "enabling them," that is, helping them avoid taking responsibility for themselves. Encouraging someone to become dependent on you is not good for either of you. When, not if, you run into this problem, encourage people to listen to their own inner voice. There are a number of books on the market that can help people learn how to get in touch with their intuition, including my own, *A Still Small Voice*. Our job as psychics is to help people understand their lives better, not to make ourselves the focus of a person's life.

Friends and Acquaintances

In the beginning of your development, you'll probably be practicing on willing friends, and it'll be fun. Lots of sharing and lots of laughs.

Then a common problem will slowly creep in: over time, your friends may start looking to you for guidance with everything in their lives. Whenever anything comes up that causes them anxiety, fear, or pain of some kind, they'll want you to tell them the outcome. Your friendships will no longer have the same give and take. You may start to feel it is all give, give, give on your part, and you might find yourself avoiding your friends altogether.

The other problem that might come up is going to social parties. If the word has gotten out that you've developed your psychic abilities, people will come up to you at parties and ask if they can "just ask one psychic question." This might seem fun at first, but it gets old very quickly.

My advice is to nip this in the bud right away. Let your friends know that when you're out socializing with them, you're there to have a good time like everyone else. Tell them to call you at a more appropriate time with their questions. Another suggestion is to get some business cards made up. Then when people approach you for some free psychic advice, hand them your business card and tell them to call to set up an appointment.

I know this sounds cold and off-putting, but this is the kind of thing that causes us to burn out. Everyone in the world has some kind of problem, and everyone wants to know how it's going to turn out. If you let yourself become the psychic ATM machine for everyone you know, you will come to resent them and your gifts.

You need to decide what you're willing to do and then set boundaries and stick to them. There will be times when your intuition is really pushing you to give someone a message, and other times you will get a definite feeling to stay out of it. Follow your intuition in these cases, not your intellect. In the long run, though, just remember that by protecting yourself, you are also protecting your friendships.

Let Your Light Shine

Do you know what the difference is between a "fortune teller" and a "prophet," *besides* psychic development and lots of practice? It's knowing that we're worthy of developing ourselves to our highest potential. It's discovering the power within ourselves and letting our light shine.

The more we step into our "Christ-consciousness shoes," the more we understand our oneness with God and discover our unlimited potential. We stop letting our fears control our lives. We stop trying to shrink ourselves to fit the same mold as everyone else. We stop playing small and accept the responsibility that comes from being an heir to God.

The wonderful role models we have today — John Edward, James Van Praagh, Sylvia Browne, George Anderson, Rosemary Altea — have all pushed themselves and gone up against the lions so that we can see what is possible. I am so grateful to these gifted psychics and mediums for developing themselves to the level that they have and showing us what's possible.

Psychically gifted people have been around since the beginning of time. Psychics and psychic abilities are not going away. In spite of what some religions teach, these are Gifts of the Spirit and should be recognized as such. The picture that pops into my third eye when I think about these gifts is the Energizer Bunny. In spite of all the obstacles, we just keep on going...

I wish you the very best on your journey, and don't forget to practice, practice, practice!

Appendix

Personal Stories of Five Gifted Psychics

The best way to understand what it's like to be psychically gifted, and what it means to live a life that honors and celebrates these gifts, is to hear psychics tell their own stories. I asked five psychics I know (and whom I recommend on my website, www.echobodine.com) to share their experiences, and I gave them a list of questions to answer. In the case of Susan Reishus, she chose to write her answers in story form.

Valerie Celene

Q: What do you physically look like?

A: I am five feet, ten inches tall and have dark brown hair, brown eyes, and an athletic build.

Q: What psychic gifts do you have?

A: I am clairvoyant, clairaudient, clairsentient, and telepathic.

Q: How old were you when you first discovered your psychic gifts?

A: I was twenty years old when I discovered that what I had been doing all my life was being psychic.

Q: How did you discover them?

A: At the time I was involved in a therapy group for women, and my therapist suggested I see a local psychic named Echo Bodine. She felt that Echo could assist me with what my therapist saw taking place in the group. She explained that several of the members had voiced their concern about the feedback I was giving people during group. They felt that I had access to more information than they were comfortable with!

Q: Did you have any signs as a child that you had these abilities?

A: My first memories of seeing spirits happened around the age of three. I can still see what the spirit looked like: she was very tall (I suppose everyone is tall to a three year old), she was standing in our living room surrounded by a pale blue light, she had long blondish hair that went past her shoulders, and I remember her smiling at me. What really stands out in this memory is the reaction of my mom when I told her to look at the pretty lady.

Q: How did you develop your abilities?

A: I went to see Echo Bodine for my first reading, at which time she helped explain a lot of what was going on in my life and suggested I take her psychic development classes.

I went on to take Echo's classes on and off for the next seven years. It was a difficult process for me. I would get terrified each time I received information in class, then I wouldn't go back to another class for a year or so!

Q: How do these abilities affect your life?

A: Every day I give thanks to the Universe for the ability to develop my Gifts of the Spirit. The process has helped me to heal in ways that I don't know I would have been able to if hadn't followed this path. Each time that I am able to work with people, I see miracles taking place. I feel my gifts have had a very positive effect on the quality of life I live. There are times, like when I am applying for a bank loan or filing legal documents, that I am asked about my occupation, and that can be a bit of a challenge!

Q: Do you read people's minds?

A: No! I prefer much more interesting reading.

Q: Do you see people's deep dark secrets when you first meet them?

A: No.

Q: Can you see when people are going to die and how?

A: No, and I wouldn't ever want to.

Q: Do you read palms?

A: No.

Q: Do you have a specialty, such as seeing the future, communicating with the dead, or reading past lives?

A: I do help people heal their relationships with loved ones on the other side. It feels like the majority of my work is helping people resolve their past, so they are able to "see" a better future for themselves. I do get information about the future, but as with anything this is very different from client to client.

Q: What hobbies or interests do you have?

A: I love and teach kick-boxing. I dance, play music, and practice yoga daily.

Q: Do you have children, and do they have these abilities?

A: I am blessed with a seven-year-old boy who has been displaying his gifts from the very beginning. He sees spirits all the
time and will often respond to a thought I have before I have
spoken it!

Q: Are you glad you have these gifts?

A: Very!

Q: What is the downside to having them?

A: I guess socially it can be difficult when people act like you have the
plague.

Q: What's the biggest misconception about psychics you'd like to
dispel?

A: We are not freaks of nature. There have always been oracles, seers,
and medicine men and women. Our gifts are a natural part of who
we are, just like a gifted artist or musician.

Q: How long did you work at developing your abilities?

A: I worked on and off for seven years before giving psychic readings
professionally.

Q: Do you use any tools in your work (such as cards) and why?

A: Yes, I choose to use crystals in my readings. I feel that their vibration helps me to stay grounded in the light personally, allowing
for me to be a stronger channel. I have always loved crystals, and
I find their beauty to be gentle reminders of spirit. I can also do
readings without the assistance of crystals, but when I have done
this, I find I do not have the same level of energy when I am done.
When working with crystals, I find my work energizing and
uplifting.

Paula Hill

Q: What do you physically look like?

A: I am slender and tall, athletic and healthy, with dark hair and light eyes.

Q: What psychic gifts do you have?

A: I am empathic and clairvoyant.

Q: How old were you when you discovered your gifts?

A: I was three or four when I knew that I had abilities that other people didn't. I recall telling adults things that would astonish them (such as, "I'm sorry that you're upset because you shouted at Mary," or "I am sorry that your head hurts," or "I'm sorry that your friend died").

Q: How did you discover them?

A: I simply began to allow them to come through without "Paula" getting in the way.

Q: How do these abilities affect your life?

A: Most people respond in fear when I talk about being a psychic. They believe that I will "read" them without permission. I have learned *not* to provide insights unless I am asked, even with my very old and dear friends. They may not be ready or able to hear and absorb the information, and therefore they become upset by it.

Q: Can you read people's minds?

A: No, I cannot read people's minds. My "job" is to work with people through their spirit guides, who communicate with my guides.

Q: Do you see people's deep dark secrets when you first meet them?

A: I do not invade people's privacy by looking at their issues, good/bad, light/dark. It would be inappropriate to read people's minds.

Q: Can you see when people are going to die?

A: When clients ask me about death, I will tell them. I can "see" at what age they agreed to pass on, when their contract, per se, ends. Sometimes I see they will have a choice, at a particular age, to continue on their path in this body or move on to the next plane.

Q: Do you read palms?

A: No, I don't.

Q: Do you have a specialty, such as seeing the future, communicating with the dead, or reading past lives?

A: I can see the future and read past lives, especially when it helps people move forward in this lifetime, such as providing insights about lessons that were not overcome in the past or how a relationship is being driven by or needs to be completed from a past life.

Q: What hobbies and interests do you have?

A: My interests and hobbies are reading, especially about the metaphysical arena; participating and watching sports, particularly volleyball and soccer; travel, both domestic and international; and spending quality time with my daughter.

Q: Do you have children, and do they have these abilities? How do you know?

A: I have an eight-year-old daughter who I "hear" is, in fact, intuitive, yet her skills and abilities are not at as high a level as mine.

Q: Are you glad you have these gifts?

A: I am extremely pleased to have been chosen to share my abilities with others.

Q: What is the downside to having these abilities?

A: The downside is that people fear the "dark side," which they may or may not understand, as well as fearing seemingly negative information.

Q: What is the biggest misconception about psychics that you'd like to dispel?

A: The biggest misconception is that mediums are "fakes."

Q: Do you use any tools in your work (such as cards) and why?

A: I do not use any tools. I just open my third eye and create a space for the information to come in and provide a listening for it. I find that tools tend to get in the way and interfere with the clarity of the information.

Q: Is there anything you would like to add?

A: Mediums, in general, are vehicles for people to gain insight into their lives, to "unstick" and move forward in spite of the fear. We are delighted to assist people, which may, in fact, unstick us in the process! It is truly a gift for me, as a psychic, as well as my clients.

Susan Reishus

My name is Susan A. Reishus, and I have been intuitive all my life. My mother and maternal grandmother have always known things, and I always prayed to have a gift as great as theirs. I am the eldest of seven children, and my siblings all have keen insight also.

With time, I realized that my father's gift was greater than all of my family put together; though he never spoke of it, he used it daily. I have two children born twenty-two years apart, and both are keenly intuitive and connected, and their abilities far outshine mine. They each use their gifts differently, based upon who they are and what they came to contribute. I must say that I am exceptionally fortunate that they chose me for a parent.

I believe we select a body and genetics that can help facilitate having our intuitive centers more open. We all are given intuition, and it is enhanced when one listens to and uses it. I have also clearly seen that one's spiritual focus, or wish to be of service to one's soul and to others, enhances one's abilities, and such people receive more Celestial assistance.

I have always had visions. If there was something I wanted to understand, they would give me a vision that would give complete clarity. There have always been High Beings around me, ever since I was born (as with many of you), and they would come to give me parts of the Plan to facilitate my being here. I had relationships with my deceased grandparents, and I would also go and astral travel to visit people I was to have relationships with decades later, to check in with them. I would consciously visit the Higher Planes and other Systems throughout my life. The first three to five years after I was born, there were many explanations of how they did things here (by High Beings from this and other Systems), to make it easier for me.

I seem to get communication in every way one recognizes. I see it all as unlimited. I am clairsentient, clairaudient, clairvoyant, and kinesthetic (can hold objects and discern much information from them). I can also smell messages, see written words outside myself or in my mind's eye, read auras, facilitate healings on various levels, speak to Hierarchy or discarnate souls or beings, diagnose medical or mental problems (by scanning the body or not), and occasionally information even comes through taste (such as, when I'm in a restaurant, I can taste the consciousness of the cook). I can hear words inside of me, outside of me, or the booming God voice when they feel it is important, too. I can dream prophetic events. I have had shamanic training by Beings from the other side. I have been given the gift of healing, hands-on or otherwise. I have had a strong connection with leaving and going to the other side, before and after my death experience. When I do readings, I align with the Highest I can and turn it over to what is in your Highest and best interest. That way I ask for the information to be clear and pure, and I feel that aligning with Spiritual/the Divine is the truest way and truly enhances one's gift. I find doing readings to be very energizing and healing. When I read, I prefer to allow the first portion for what Higher Guidance has to say before taking questions, as it is easier for me and more meaningful to the client. My main focus for the past twenty-five years has been on the Soul. The readings are meant to be at least helpful, and for some they are life-changing. My hope is that it is a very important hour of your life and a chance to connect with the other side to validate or make things clear and smoother for you.

Being intuitive can be a challenge, as you can pick up energies that people throw out there when you are going to the store or driving on the freeway. Going to antique stores, bars, or airports can be particularly difficult. This can be adjusted easily by remembering to stay in your Soul/Center. When meeting people, I try to tune out, as I feel that people's privacy is to be respected, but at times I get a tap on the shoulder to say something to someone. One can often see when people are to die and how, and that energy can be overwhelmingly strong (as it is for the person who is about to die) a day or two before, and they can appear to be more translucent. I can read palms, and I have some remembrance of a past life when I knew how to read the hands and fingernails, particularly, and faces and ears. I prefer not to use facilitators, and I have never used tarot cards, or other methods of scrying, when doing a reading.

I am five feet, ten inches tall, with chestnut brown hair and blue eyes. I love doing all forms of needlework and sewing, as well as writing and painting, as they are creative and give one meditation and "direct connection" time. Then the mind is busy and in more of a receptive listening state. I feel that we are all given gifts to use to facilitate our own Path and the Path of others to make things the way they were intended to be. The vision includes raising the consciousness of the planet and our bodies and our awareness to be Ascended, with manifested Love, Joy, Harmony, and Peace. May you awaken to your Soul's Purpose for being here and Divine Blessings to You and Yours! What an exciting time to be here!

Sunni Welles

Q: What do you physically look like?

A: I think God has blessed me to have an attractive appearance. My weight is well proportioned for my height, which is five feet, five inches. My eyes are green but sometimes hazel — they tend to change color occasionally. My hair color has gone from its natural dark brown to auburn and red (when I wanted a change), to blond (when I really wanted a change), and now back to a medium brown color to bring out the green of my eyes. My best features, I have been told, are my smile, my eyes, and my expressiveness.

Q: What psychic gifts do you have?

A: Automatic handwriting, clairaudience, and clairvoyance.

Q: How old were you when you first discovered your psychic gifts?

A: About seven years old, as I recall. But I did not put much thought into it at the time or for many years afterward — not until I asked to be of service to God and saw what occurred after my prayer.

Q: How did you discover them?

A: I became aware of unusual circumstances after I prayed fervently to God to be of service to him.

Q: Did you have any signs as a child that you had these abilities?

A: Yes, but as mentioned above, I did not acknowledge them at the time.

Q: How did you develop your abilities?

A: I did nothing to develop them per se, but I just allowed God to use me for his will.

Q: How many years did you work at developing your abilities, before becoming a psychic?

A: Actually, I never had to work to develop my gifts. I hope that I don't sound proud, because I say it with a tone of reverence and humility. My first gifts came all at once, shortly after I prayed a fervent and specific prayer asking God to please use me in service to him. My gifts were increased over the years when God must have thought I was ready to do and know more. I did ask, following the receipt of my gifts, that only God's will be done in the use of my gifts. This is one of the reasons why I give God the glory for everything. I had nothing to do with my gifts or their development. My gifts are blessings, and I mention this every chance I get because I am so filled with gratitude to God for giving me the most fulfilling work I have ever been blessed to do.

Q: How do these abilities affect your life?

A: It is the most fulfilling work I have ever done — being able to help the bereaved and the grieving, and to help the angels of God write their book through my hand. My life is full of very good friends of like mind, and the circle is ever widening as I gain new clients from others' referrals to me. A total blessing.

Q: Do you read people's minds?

A: Sometimes thoughts will come to me from people, but I do not speak to them about it. It is not something I try to do. It just happens.

Q: Do you see people's deep dark secrets when you first meet them?

A: I may receive some information about a person occasionally, but I do not put much thought into wanting to know someone's personal and private information.

Q: Can you see when people are going to die and how?

A: No, I am not able to do this, but I do have friends who have this gift. I'm grateful, though, that I do not have this particular gift. I think God knew that I would be too sensitive if I were able to see

170

this. I'd worry too much and feel too sad for the family of the person who was going to pass.

Q: Do you read palms?

A: No, I have no interest in palmistry.

Q: Do you have a specialty such as seeing the future, communicating with the dead, or reading past lives?

A: I primarily communicate with spirits who have passed on. I am also able to reach a person's angels.

Q: What hobbies or interests do you have?

A: Many, but I have little time for them, unfortunately. I love to sing, and jazz is my most favorite style to sing. I have an extensive background in show business, and I was on the road as an entertainer for over thirty years.

Q: Do you have children, and do they have these abilities? How do you know?

A: If my only son has these abilities, he has not spoken to me about it. The gifts I use in my life now were given to me after my son was grown and moved out of the house.

Q: Are you glad you have these gifts?

A: I feel absolutely blessed in every way.

Q: What is the downside to having them?

A: Generally, there is no downside for me — except possibly that I must occasionally deal with naysayers and skeptics and the negative emails they sometimes send.

Q: What's the biggest misconception about psychics you'd like to dispel?

A: Well, I do not consider myself psychic but rather a medium who is in grief and bereavement support. I think, though, that there might be a whole collective misconception on our planet that what all psychics and mediums do is "bunk" and that we're self-serving snake oil salespeople. I'd say that there probably is about as much fraud in our business as in any other profession. The best way for a person to find a reputable medium or psychic is to try to find one through a referral.

Q: Do you use any tools in your work (such as cards) and why?

A: Nope, just God's gift. That's all I need.

Q: What would you like to add?

A: I'd like to thank God for the gifts that he, from his love and mercy, has given me to use for his glory and for the benefit of others in finding comfort and peace. I appreciate so much having God, Christ, and his Holy Spirit in my life to guide me and expand me as a human being and spiritual soul. I would also like to add that I have been blessed to learn that life and love are absolutely ongoing and unending, which is the most wonderful blessing (in my estimation) that God has given us — after, of course, the blessing to our soul life of the sacrifice of his Son. How truly *blessed* we are.

Beverly Williams

Q: What do you physically look like?

A: I am five feet, one inch tall and one hundred pounds, with blonde hair and green eyes.

Q: What psychic gifts do you have?

A: I am clairvoyant, clairaudient, clairsentient, and a medium. I also see energy (auras) and am a spiritual healer.

Q: How old were you when you first discovered your psychic gifts?

A: As long as I can remember, I've been psychic. I just didn't realize what it was when I was very young. I knew I was different, but I didn't understand how.

Q: How did you discover them?

A: I would know things about people and would also hear spirits who were connected to people.

Q: Did you have any signs as a child that you had these abilities?

A: My strongest memory as a child was knowing that I wasn't alone, even though I couldn't see anyone. I felt like I was always being watched, which made me aware of spirit guides.

Q: How did you develop your abilities?

A: When I was in my early twenties, my gifts started to greatly increase, and I realized I needed to learn how to control them and set boundaries with spirits. For many years, I read and studied constantly, took classes, and prayed about it. Most of all, practice, practice.

Q: How long did you work at developing your gifts?

A: Although I've been psychic most of my life, I studied probably five years before I started doing readings professionally. And, as you know, the studies didn't end there — they always continue. As you grow, your readings change and get more refined. Also, your guides may change (which happened to me several years ago), and it's a new level of information that I receive.

Q: How do these abilities affect your life?

A: For the most part, I am able to turn it off when I'm not working. But sometimes, it comes through anyway. Also, there is still such a stigma attached to being psychic; people are afraid of it or think that you know everything about them.

Q: Do you read people's minds?

A: Generally, no. But sometimes it does happen. I hear people thinking questions and respond to them before they speak.

Q: Do you see people's deep dark secrets when you first meet them?

A: Again, when I'm not working, I don't want to know things about other people, but sometimes I tend to get what their issues are.

Q: Can you see when people are going to die and how?

A: No. And I've never wanted to. Although, I do get some medical information regarding health conditions, but that's different.

Q: Do you read palms?

A: No, straight psychic abilities.

Q: Do you have a specialty such as seeing the future, communicating with the dead, or reading past lives?

A: In my readings, I specialize in looking at current life issues and problems and receiving information (past life, and so on) as to when/where they started and how they can be healed.

Q: What hobbies or interests do you have?

A: Music, reading, movies, walking, cooking, and decorating.

Q: Do you have children, and do they have these abilities?

A: I have a twenty-year-old son who is very sensitive psychically, but doesn't feel connected to it. I feel he will come into it later in life.

Q: Are you glad you have these gifts?

A: I've always said, these gifts choose you, you don't choose them. I am generally happy with my gifts and the ability to help people, but sometimes it is more responsibility than I would like.

Q: What is the downside to having them?

A: The expectations of some people are too great. It is not an exact science, and it's hard for people to understand that. Usually, I surpass their expectations, but sometimes people are looking to hear certain things, and when you tell them differently (truth), they rebel. Some people are also looking for someone to tell them what to do, and I would never do this. I work to empower, not dominate.

Q: What's the biggest misconception about psychics you'd like to dispel?

A: The biggest myth is that psychics know *everything*. This is simply very far from the truth. We have an enhanced view of situations and people, but don't have all the answers. The other common myth is that we will tell them something bad (like they are going to die).

Q: Do you use any tools in your work (such as cards) and why?

A: No. For me, tools are distracting.

Q: What would you like to add?

A: I would like to stress that going to a reputable psychic can be very helpful in getting the information that helps people heal and make better choices in their lives. But I also want to emphasize that everyone has spirit guides, and if people just ask for help, it will come.

Recommended Reading

Altea, Rosemary. *The Eagle and the Rose: A Remarkable True Story.* New York: Warner Books, 1996. To order, call 800-759-0190; also available on audiocassette.

———. *You Own the Power: Stories and Exercises to Inspire and Unleash the Force Within.* New York: HarperCollins, 2001. Also available on audiocassette.

Beattie, Melody. *Choices: Taking Control of Your Life and Making It Matter.* San Francisco: HarperSanFrancisco, 2002.

———. *Codependent No More: How to Stop Controlling Others and Start Caring for Yourself.* San Francisco: HarperSanFrancisco, 1996.

Choquette, Sonia. *The Psychic Pathway: A Workbook for Reawakening the Voice of Your Soul.* New York: Carol Trade Paperbacks, 1995.

Edward, John. *Developing Your Own Psychic Powers.* Carlsbad, Calif.: Hay House, 2000. Audiocassette. Order from www.hayhouse.com or by calling 800-654-5126.

———. *One Last Time: A Psychic Medium Speaks to Those We Have*

Loved and Lost. New York: Berkeley Books, 1998. A workbook section helps you tune into your own psychic abilities.

Marion, Jim. *Putting on the Mind of Christ: The Inner Work of Christian Spirituality.* Charlottesville, Va.: Hampton Roads Publishing, 2002.

Mesich, Kyra. *Modern Meditation: Going Within.* Minneapolis, Minn.: Self-Published, 2000. This and Dr. Mesich's other self-published book can be ordered from www.kyramesich.com.

———. *The Sensitive Person's Survival Guide.* Minneapolis, Minn.: Ansuz Press, 2000.

Owens, Elizabeth. *How to Communicate with Spirits.* St. Paul, Minn.: Llewellyn Publications, 2001.

Patterson, Doris T., and Violet M. Shelley. *Be Your Own Psychic.* Virginia Beach, Va.: Edgar Cayce Foundation, 1991. Based on the Edgar Cayce readings.

Reed, Henry. *Awakening Your Psychic Powers: An Edgar Cayce Guide.* New York: St. Martin's Press, 1996. How to open your inner mind and control your psychic intuition.

Sanders, Pete A., Jr. *You are Psychic!* New York: Fawcett Books, 1990. An MIT-trained scientist's proven program for expanding your psychic powers.

Van Praagh, James. *Heaven and Earth: Making the Psychic Connection.* New York: Simon & Schuster, 2001. Includes exercises; also available on audiocassette.

Webster, Richard. *Aura Reading for Beginners: Develop Your Psychic Awareness for Health and Success.* St. Paul, Minn.: Llewellyn Publications, 1998.

About the Author

E cho Bodine is a renowned psychic, spiritual healer, and teacher. She has appeared on many national television programs, including NBC's *Later Today, Sally Jesse Raphael, Sightings,* and *The Other Side.* She is the author of several books about psychic and spiritual phenomena, including *Echoes of the Soul; Hands That Heal; A Still, Small Voice; Relax, It's Only a Ghost;* and *Dear Echo.*

Echo lectures throughout the country on life, death, life after death, living by intuition, and developing psychic abilities. She can be reached at:

Post Office Box 385321
Bloomington, MN 55438
echo@echobodine.com

Visit Echo's website for information about her books, videos, and tapes:

Echobodine.com

If you enjoyed *The Gift*, we recommend the following books and audio books from New World Library:

The Art of True Healing by Israel Regardie. This book centers around a very powerful meditation exercise — called the Middle Pillar — through which one can stimulate body, mind, and spirit. Through this technique, readers will learn to focus energy in a variety of ways for improving their health, success, and ability to help others.

Creative Visualization by Shakti Gawain. The classic work (in print for twenty-five years, three million copies sold) that shows us how to use the power of our imagination to create what we want in life. Available on audio as well, in two formats: the complete book on tape, and selected meditations from the book.

Developing Intuition by Shakti Gawain. Through simple exercises, Shakti Gawain shows us step-by-step way to develop our intuitive ability. We learn to sense the difference between intuitive feelings and emotions, and to distinguish our intuitive voice from our many other inner voices.

Living in the Light: A Guide to Personal and Planetary Transformation (Revised) by Shakti Gawain, with Laurel King. A newly updated edition of the recognized classic on developing intuition and using it as a guide in living your life.

Miracles of Mind by Russel Targ and Jane Katra, Ph.D. In this inspiring exploration of the mind's power, pioneering physicist Russel Targ and spiritual healer Jane Katra explore how our mind's ability to transcend the limits of time and space is linked to our capacity for healing.

The Nature of Personal Reality by Jane Roberts. Seth explains how the conscious mind directs unconscious activity and has at its command all the powers of the inner self.

The Path of Transformation: How Healing Ourselves Can Change the World by Shakti Gawain. Shakti describes how to effect powerful change in personal lives and how we can all make a difference in the world.

Seth Speaks by Jane Roberts. In this essential guide to conscious living, Seth clearly and powerfully articulates the concept that we create our own reality according to our beliefs.

The Seven Spiritual Laws of Success by Deepak Chopra. A practical guide to the fulfillment of your dreams. An international bestseller, and for a very good reason. Available on audio as well.

Seven Whispers by Christina Baldwin. In this eloquent work Christina Baldwin shares the wisdom gained from listening to the voice of her inner spirit. Each chapter centers on a meditative phrase: "Maintain peace of mind," "Move at the pace of guidance," "Practice certainty of purpose," "Surrender to surprises," "Ask for what you need and offer what you can," "Love the folks in front of you," and "Return to the world."

Simple Truths by Kent Nerburn. Clear and gentle guidance on the big issues in life. Elegant, profound, and inspiring.

Signals by Joel Rothschild. This book is the true story of two friends, both living with AIDS, who made a pact: whomever died first would try to contact the other. Joel Rothschild, the more skeptical of the two, was the one left behind. His book chronicles a series of miraculous experiences and encounters that offer wonderful proof of an afterlife.

New World Library is dedicated to publishing
books and audio projects that inspire and challenge us to improve
the quality of our lives and our world.

Our books and tapes are available
in bookstores everywhere.
For a catalog of our complete library
of fine books and cassettes, contact:

New World Library
14 Pamaron Way
Novato, CA 94949

Phone: (415) 884-2100
Fax: (415) 884-2199
Or call toll-free (800) 972-6657
Catalog requests: Ext. 50
Ordering: Ext. 52

E-mail: escort@nwlib.com
www.newworldlibrary.com